The Urbana Free Library

To renew materials call
217-367-4057

UNSETTLED

ALSO BY MARC ARONSON:

RACE: A History Beyond Black and White
WITCH-HUNT: Mysteries of the Salem Witch Trials

MARC ARONSON

ginee seo books
atheneum books for young readers
NEW YORK LONDON TORONTO SYDNEY

UNSETTLED

The PROBLEM of LOVING ISRAEL

FOR GINEE SEO

Atheneum Books for Young Readers
An imprint of Simon & Schuster Children's Publishing Division
1230 Avenue of the Americas, New York, New York 10020
Copyright © 2008 by Marc Aronson
Book design by Michael McCartney
The text for this book is set in Requiem.
Manufactured in the United States of America
First Edition
10 9 8 7 6 5 4 3 2 1
CIP data for this book is available from the Library of Congress.
ISBN-13: 978-1-4169-1261-3
ISBN-10: 1-4169-1261-4

CONTENTS

V. HOW CAN ISRAEL BE A STRONG STATE, A JEWISH HOMELAND, AND TRULY DEMOCRATIC?

Foreword

I love Israel.

Israel protected my father's parents and six of his brothers and sisters from Russian thugs and Communist murderers. Israel sheltered three of my mother's cousins from the Nazis. Israel harbored one of my wife's South American cousins and rescued a long list of in-laws from Jew haters in Iraq, Turkey, Yemen, and beyond. Israel gave my family a refuge and a home.

Alongside other Israelis, these members of my family created a beautiful land. Israel truly is beautiful in every sense of the word. So much of it resembles the most blessed landscapes of California—places where even the air feels golden. But the beauty is not just a gift of nature. Israel is beautiful for how well the Israelis have treated the land. In just sixty years, they really have made the desert bloom. They have filled brown hills with appealing homes, playgrounds, schools, and blue, inviting, Olympic-size swimming pools. They have excavated ancient caves, forts, and temples and opened them to the public. The young county is a nurturing mother and a fertile soil, a home for its citizens, and a homeland for Jews throughout the world.

And yet I could not live in Israel.

In the 1920s, when his parents and most of his siblings moved to Palestine, my father came to America. I was always grateful that he made that choice. Frankly, it was easier for me to be a Jewish New Yorker than an Israeli. I was too scared to live in a tiny Jewish nation open to the hatred of so many in the world. But that is only part of the truth. In fact, I cannot live in Israel because it does not feel right to me. Israel was founded on principles I do not agree with, and it is being distorted by those beliefs to this day.

Strange as this sounds, my problem with Israel is related to those gorgeous swimming pools. I wrote my last book, *Race*, because of an experience I had at my local pool, when I had to admit to myself a moment of prejudice against a young black male. When I was last in Israel, I mentioned to a class of bright and lively Jewish high school students that I'd heard about an Arab citizen of Israel who had to go to court to be allowed into their local pool. The students agreed with the codes banning Arabs. "Arabs are different," one said. "They're not like us," another added. One tall thin girl explained, "I feel how the men are looking at me, I'm not comfortable."

Arab citizens of Israel* are not the Palestinians you hear about blowing themselves up in Israeli cities. Rather, they are Muslims and Christians whose families have been in Israel since the state was formed sixty years ago—and some of whose families have lived in the same villages for hundreds of years, if not more. Few Americans know

---

*In this book I will sometimes say "Arab citizen of Israel"—the term many Arabs prefer—or sometimes "Israeli Arab," which is easier to write and is itself sometimes used by Arabs. The debate over which term is appropriate is similar to the political conflicts in America over saying "black" or "African American," "Indian" or "Native American," "Latino" or "Hispanic." For the reasons behind the tensions in Israel over what to call its Arab citizens, see page 151.

A family of Arab citizens of Israel near Kisra in the Western Galilee. Israel faces the challenge of deciding whether it is, can be, or should be, a Jewish state when 23 percent of its citizens are, like these children, not Jewish.

this, but 19.6 percent of Israelis, one out of every five, is an Arab; Arabs make up a larger minority in Israel than either African Americans or Hispanics do in the United States.

Only in a few rare and isolated cases have Israeli Arabs shown disloyalty to the state of Israel. Three attacks in Jerusalem in 2008 were carried out by Arab men from the part of the city Israel captured in 1967. They are not the Arab citizens of Israel I am discussing. Every police officer and government security service agrees: Israeli Arabs are not secret allies of Israel's enemies. Indeed, Israeli Arabs vote in elections, and not only have representatives in Israel's legislature, but have—in one case—served as a minister in the Israeli government. Yet to the teenagers I spoke to, Israel is a Jewish state, so Israeli Jews can wear blinders and simply not see their neighbors.

Israelis teenagers are forthright. They tell you what they think. After graduation almost all of those high school students will go into the army, and they have been training for that ever since they were small. It is as if the whole country were one giant Outward Bound camp, designed to prepare young people to be independent so that they can face any danger. Americans pride themselves on their self-reliance, but Israeli teenagers have a maturity, a self-possession you don't always see here. They know no one else will do things for them. But that very trust-your-own-judgment mentality also means they are very open about their prejudices.

The young people in that class viewed Israeli Arabs as being so different from themselves that they must be avoided, kept apart, perhaps invited to leave the country. The students' views were not a product of actual conflicts with Arab citizens of Israel. Just the opposite: experiences of a lifetime in which the teenagers have been subject to Arab attacks from outside Israel, and in which they have had only

4

minimal contact with their Arab neighbors within Israel, had hardened into a kind of emotional wall. For a second I envied the students' lack of self-doubt, but then I knew I didn't belong.

As much as I love Israel, I am, at heart, an integrationist who trusts in a society linked by shared laws and principles, not one defined by one religion or race. I do not feel at home in a land where so many people find safety in ignoring or excluding their fellow citizens. In Israel, 92 percent of the land is owned by the state, which strongly favors Jewish settlement and is extremely slow to give any to legal, peaceful Arab citizens. As a result, while the Israeli Arabs make up 20 percent of the population, they control just 4 percent of the land. In America we would call that both unwarranted governmental control and illegal discrimination.

Of course Israelis face real dangers from their Arab neighbors, and America has its own deep current of racism and prejudice. But except for extremists, no one here would argue that the races ought to be separate, or that this should be a white country. It has been more than 150 years since any white politician advocated sending African Americans back to Africa. (From Marcus Garvey in the 1920s to black nationalists in the 1960s, some blacks have made that case, but that is a different issue.) All over Israel, people say the nation must be a Jewish state, and Avigdor Lieberman, who, until recently, was a government minister, wants to engineer a land swap so that the Arabs will be entirely removed from the Israeli population. While Lieberman wants to ensure that Israel is entirely Jewish, he and others also favor building Jewish settlements in land taken over by Israel in 1967—treating the Palestinians who live there as if they did not exist.

The strange paradox about Israel is that for a Jew—indeed, for

The Arabs whose families remained within Israel in 1948, out for a trip in Western Galilee. Some Israeli Jews believe Israeli Arabs should be encouraged to leave Israel when a Palestinian state finally takes shape, while others fight for Arab rights, seeing them as fellow citizens of a more inclusive Israel.

most Europeans or Americans of any faith—it is so warm, so beautiful, such a comfortable place to be, and yet there is a barrier separating its peoples. As an American, safe here thousands of miles away, I have no right to criticize Israelis. But, in fact, Israelis themselves are the most eloquent about what Professor David Shulman of Hebrew University calls the "violence of heart and mind" that he sees spreading among his fellow Jews.

Israel turned fifty ten years ago. That was a moment of pure celebration when we justly honored what the Israelis had achieved. But now, at sixty, when Israeli Jews themselves speak about the rights of Israeli Arabs, and the needs, the suffering, of Palestinians, it is time for an outsider to speak up. The very word "Israel" can be read as meaning "arguing with God." So this book is me arguing with God, and with myself, over what Israel is, what it was, what it could be. I owe this gift to Israel. I love the country so much I have to find out why I find it so unsettling.

So often discussions about Israel are debates between spokesmen—Mr. Israel and Mr. Palestinian. I hope that this book offers something else. I am an American Jew who could have been an Israeli had I joined my relatives there. I have visited Israel often but never lived there. I don't know what it is like to experience the constant threats Israeli Jews must endure. But I have the advantage of seeing Israel through American eyes—perhaps your eyes.

I believe that Israel and America have something fundamental in common: Both nations emerged from bloody combat in which cold strategy and deadly weapons ruled. But we are also products of the highest ideals of human conscience and heart. We are both hard and soft. That is why I hope I, and all of us as Americans, have something to offer. We don't have to blindly defend Israel or ruthlessly attack it—we can see it as we see ourselves. That is what I have tried to do in this book.

I am talking about Israel, but really I am speaking about something else: What does it mean to be a Jew? Where can a Jew feel safe? Where can a Jew feel proud? What does it mean to be Jewish? To go to synagogue? (Most Israelis don't.) To know the history of Judaism? (Most American Jews don't.) To be shaped by the memory of the Holocaust? Young people all over the world read Anne Frank and know about the camps. To be the child of a Jewish mother? In these days of intermarriage, how meaningful is that?

As an American Jew writing about Israel, I am really asking myself what it means to be Jewish today. What does America mean to us, what does Israel mean to us, what is our future? These are questions for all readers, because they are also about how the majority and minority can best relate anywhere—black and white in America, Muslim and Jew in Israel. What gives a minority a home, a sense of belonging, a place to grow and flourish? In the twenty-first century, as parents move from one country to another looking for better lives for their families, as children grow up between cultures, my questions about Israel and America, about being Jewish, are everyone's questions.

I hope my struggling over how to understand Israel's history, and Israel today, allows you, readers, to explore your own feelings. I hope I can introduce you to some points of view that get lost in the shouting. You don't have to choose a side. You don't have to line up and echo one view or another. You can join in the argument with me. Maybe that is the special gift I have as a Jew: I know that being good is not just obeying God, it is also arguing with him (or her, but that is a different argument).

❧   ❧   ❧

The first problem with criticizing Israel is that it has so many critics already; indeed, there is something about tiny, hardworking Israel that makes it a focus for the world's hatred. Speaking now as a Jew, it is easy to see that the state of Israel is much like the Jewish people throughout history—we have always been a small minority who nonetheless drew attention to ourselves—by being different, following our own rules, making money, being valued by the great and powerful. Over and over someone in the majority has decided to crush the Jews, to sweep away this annoying obstruction.

Every day, Israeli Jews experience the sour envy of an angry world, and, as if that were not enough, attacking tiny Israel is a convenient way to lash out indirectly at its giant ally, the United States. I could easily list recent incidents in France, Kenya, Russia, and the Caribbean in which an ambitious speaker, a rising militant leader, even a foulmouthed comedian, roused a crowd by spitting bile at Israel. I am certain that a great deal of the criticism of Israel is based either on an anti-Semitic bias, or is propaganda, used by politicians and nations whose own crimes at least equal, and often far outweigh, Israel's. But it is an old debater's trick to dismiss a criticism by attacking the critic, and I can't settle for that kind of easy answer. So the very force of the rage directed against Israel leads to my first question: Why do so many people hate Israel?

Introduction

WHY DO SO MANY PEOPLE—AND NATIONS—
HATE ISRAEL?

"Everyone hates us," you hear people in Israel say all the time. "The Arabs hate us. The Iranians hate us. All Muslims everywhere hate us. The smug British and anti-Semitic Europeans hate us. Everybody hates us and wishes we did not exist. We have to be strong and rely on ourselves. We can never forget the power of all that hatred. Look at Hitler—he did what everyone else would do, if they had the chance. The proof is that everyone else let him do it."

A lot of people do hate the Jews of Israel. Just about every day, rockets drop on the country. Terrorists devote their lives to bombing, suicide bombing, or otherwise harming Israelis. Go to the website of the International Middle East Media Center, which is run by Jewish and Palestinian journalists and aims to be evenhanded in its reporting (the site lists all casualties caused by both sides), and you can see the relentless pace of the carnage. Right now, someone in the world is trying to figure out how to set off a nuclear bomb in Tel Aviv. Some Israel haters really do not care that their homelands would be turned

Rescue teams evacuating casualties from the scene of a suicide terrorist attack on a no. 18 bus in Jerusalem at the intersection of Sarei Yisrael and Jaffa Streets.

into radioactive deserts if they attacked Israel with a nuclear bomb. The satisfaction of murdering so many Jews, inflicting so much damage on the state of Israel, is enough for them.

Speak to any Israeli Jew, and within minutes he or she will be talking about the threat of a nuclear-armed Iran. Leave out the nuclear bomb for a second. There are millions of people who really want Israel gone. And they hold out a promise to everyone else: If you don't want terrorism; if you don't want attacks on the World Trade Center in New York City, subways in London, trains in Madrid; if you want a safe world, then just stop protecting little troublesome Israel. What is Israel to you? In effect that is what terrorists say to non-Jews everywhere. Just give it up and your life will be better.

Given that so many people are so angry, is there some fundamental problem with Israel? Would the world be better off without a Jewish state? Or is the problem just that Israel is located in the Middle East? Could the Jews of Israel get up and move to New York, Toronto, or London? Why are the Jews in Israel anyway? Even in Israel, speaking to Jewish teenagers, I heard these questions. So to answer that first question about why Israel is so hated, we need to turn to history and explain how Israel came to be.

I. How Did Israel Come to Be?

HOLY LAND

The modern state of Israel was born on May 14, 1948. But why? Why did a new nation come to be—there, at that time, with the goal being a Jewish state? You might think the answers to this rest in thousands of years of history—and I'll get to that in a moment. But there was something very particular about the much more recent past that led to the creation of Israel. As much as Israel is an ancient land, as a nation it is the product of changes in the world that began in the late 1800s.

At that time, the strongest power in the area of what is now Israel was the Ottoman Empire. Based in Turkey, the Ottomans ruled much of what we now call the Middle East. When Ottomans took over the region in the 1500s, they did not agonize over the rights of the Mameluks they conquered, just as the Mameluks had no hesitation about overrunning the Ayubbids, who had themselves defeated the prior victors, and so on back beyond recorded time. When one conqueror lost, the next strong power took over.

The Ottomans were Muslims, but not Arabs. Islam, the religion of the Muslims, is a faith anyone can join. In fact, part of the appeal of Islam is the brotherhood it offers to all peoples. The Ottomans were Turks and they ruled over the Arabs, non-Arab Muslims, Christians, and Jews who lived in Palestine. Muslims living in the area of Palestine had no reason to think of forming a nation of their own. From their point of view, if they were part of a larger unit, it was their particular family or clan, or the broad union of all Muslims, or of all Arabs, or of the peoples of the Ottoman Empire.

Sari Nusseibeh, for example, is a modern Palestinian professor of philosophy whose memoir, *Once Upon a Country,* I will refer to again and again. He traces his roots to a female ancestor who fought beside Mohammed and her brother, who was given the key to the Church of the Holy Sepulcher when the Muslims conquered Jerusalem in AD 638. When Sari was growing up, the lineage of the Nusseibehs defined who they were far more than their allegiance to any state or government.

When Mark Twain visited the Holy Land in 1867, the region looked terrible to him: a "hopeless, dreary, heart-broken land." Apparently, no one lived there. "There is not a solitary village throughout its whole extent—not for thirty miles in either direction. . . . One may ride ten miles hereabouts and not see ten human beings." Some Jews have seized on this as proof that Palestine was empty before the modern Jews arrived. But they are surely wrong. Historians estimate that about four hundred thousand Arabs, Muslims, and Christians actually lived there at the time. I suspect Twain's words are a response to how people lived their lives.

Twain had grown up amid American hustle and bustle, paddle-wheel steamers going up and down the Mississippi, hopeful miners rushing out west. The nation he knew was just entering the age of the railroad and the factory; it was the world center of ambition and drive. The Holy Land was a place of heat and dust where there was none of that energy. You could tell you were coming to an Arab village when you saw olive trees—whose branches always look ancient and wizened, like the bent backs and thin arms of old, old men—and spiky clumps of cactus plants. Every village had its flocks of goats, and generations of hungry animals had eaten away all the grass cover. The hills were brown, the pace slow. Even land near water, which might have been used for farming, was swampy—a perfect breeding ground for malaria.

Where there was good land, a Jewish commentator noticed thirty years after Twain, an Arab was sure to be working it. Sari's mother's family, for example, kept lush, fragrant orange groves. But in general people did not come to this dusty, dry region to farm. They came to pray. There were villages and even cities when Twain arrived, but they were not organized around business, like New York or St. Louis or San Francisco. Instead, Muslims, Jews, as well as every variety of Christian, lived near holy sites, many of which were (and are) in Jerusalem.

Jerusalem is so central to Jews, Christians, and Muslims that it is unlike any other place on Earth. According to some traditions, it was the site of the Garden of Eden, and Adam himself was buried there. Observant Jews believe that Abraham brought his son Isaac to a hill in Jerusalem to be sacrificed, before God told him not to; the last Jewish temple stood on that same site, before the Romans destroyed it in AD 70, leaving only one wall of the larger building complex standing. Jews outside of Israel, remembering the pain of having their homeland destroyed, call that wall the Wailing Wall. Jews in Israel, feeling they are creating a modern Jewish homeland, call it the Western Wall. Christians believe Jesus, carrying his cross, suffered his last hours walking through the streets of Jerusalem before he was crucified near that very hill, and his body was buried in the Church of the Holy Sepulcher. When the Muslims arrived, they built their great mosque, the Dome of the Rock, on the same hill, to announce that theirs was the last and greatest of the faiths. Devout Muslims believe that Mohammed visited that very site in his Night Journey, and ascended from there to heaven, where he met Abraham and the other prophets before returning to Earth.

To this day you can walk from the dome to the church to the wall in less than five minutes. When Twain visited, the faithful at these sacred places were paying attention to their prayers to God, not to the world around them. The Holy Land was a collection of sites sacred to various faiths, not anything like a country. But even as Twain wrote about his journey, the age of empires was drawing to a close, and the era of nations was beginning.

NATIONALISM

Go to a major sports event anywhere in the world, and you will probably hear the country's national anthem before the game begins. If you could understand the words, you'd hear a major difference between the way we Americans define our country and the way many others, on every continent, define themselves. The United States is the nation of all those who agree to its laws. We sing of America as the "land of the free and the home of the brave"—not the "land of the whites" or the "home of the Christians." But in the 1800s, a very different idea of what a nation should be was taking shape in Europe: ethnic nationalism. Nationalists believe that every people that has its own language, religion, culture—some would say even its own race—needs a separate home. In a nationalist vision, patriotism is about the love of *a* homeland for *a* people.

The national anthem of modern Saudi Arabia, for example, says, "O my country,/My country, may you always live,/The glory of all Muslims!" In turn, the Polish national anthem expresses Christian sentiments: "O Mother of God, Virgin blessed by God, Maria!/With your son, our Lord, O mother chosen, Maria!/Intercede for us, send Him to us." And even peaceful Denmark, in its national anthem, makes very clear who are and are not Danes: "King Christian stood by the tall mast in smoke and mist; his sword was hammering so hard that the Swedes' helmets and brains cracked." In all of these nations, who you are, which God you worship, matters more than whether you are "free" or "brave."

The Jewish form of nationalism is called Zionism, the yearning to create a Jewish homeland in the ancient land of the Jewish people. And that is where the Bible, and ancient history, and the long exile of Jews from their homeland comes into play. To Jews, to believers in the Bible, the physical land of Israel was given by divine promise to the children of Abraham. In the Bible, God commands Abraham, who was living in what is now Iraq, "Get thee out of thy country . . . unto a land that I will show thee; and I will make of thee a great nation, and I will bless thee, and make thy name great." Abraham listens, and takes his wife and family to "the land of Canaan." There, God says, "unto thy seed will I give this land."

God gives Abraham a mission, promises him a special place in the world, and assures him that not only his own family, but "a great nation" will take root in what is now Israel. Indeed, even after being enslaved in Egypt, Moses leads the Jews back to that special place.

Both Jews, who trace their ancestry to Abraham's son Isaac, and Arabs, who believe their ancestor was Abraham's son Ishmael, see their claim to Israel in this biblical story.

To modern eyes, of course, there is no proof that any of this is true. We don't know if there was an Abraham, whether he or any such ancestor of the Jews ever moved to Canaan, or why. And I find it senseless to debate whether modern Palestinians are direct descendents of Ishmael or of ancient Caananites, Phoenicians, Philistines, Hittites, or of more recent Egyptian immigrants. In fact, the most sophisticated DNA tests show that European Jews and modern Palestinians are genetically nearly identical. Rational questions, though, do not diminish the power that these ancient writings have had over Jews, Christians, and Muslims for thousands of years. It was not until the late 1800s that believers in these three great religions seriously began to question the accuracy of the Bible. And, to this day, some assert that the Bible is the literal word of God.

Both the Bible and the historical record tell us that the Jews were not able to remain content in their homeland. Their temple was destroyed, and they were taken in captivity to Babylon (in what is now Iraq). Then, after Jews were allowed to return and build a second temple, they clashed with the Romans. In AD 70 the terrible armies of Rome marched to Jerusalem and demolished the Second Temple. From then on, Jews slowly scattered throughout the Mediterranean, the Roman Empire, and the whole world. Still, no matter where they lived, and no matter how much they were persecuted or oppressed, they kept alive the hope that someday, someday, they would be reunited with their fellow Jews, and would, once again, live as "a great nation" in the land God had promised to them.

Jews were a dispersed people—a diaspora—scattered in countries all over the world, always a small minority that made an easy target for superstitious neighbors, or greedy nobles, or kings who preferred not to pay their debts. Whether through threats or enticements, Jews were under constant pressure to convert—to give up their faith. And yet the Jews did not yield, did not convert, and did not die out.

Jews held on to the hope that someday, they would join together again as a people in the land of Israel. Every single year at Passover, the holiday in which Jews celebrate their escape from slavery in Egypt, Jews throughout the world say to one another, "Next year in Jerusalem." Next year, God willing—next year if the king stops his talk of taking our possessions, if the peasants hold off their attacks, if the priests stop telling lies about us killing Christian babies, if our sons and daughters are safe—next year we will meet again in Jerusalem. "Hatikvah," which became the national anthem of Israel, captures this dream:

> *Our hope is not yet lost,*
> *The hope of two thousand years.*
> *To be a free people in our land,*
> *The land of Zion and Jerusalem.*

The Jewish yearning to return to Israel was a special form of nationalism. It was an ache for the life of exile to end, for a new life to begin in which Jews could hold their heads high. Some Jews felt that, because they were always a minority, they were developing bad traits: seeing themselves as physically and mentally weak; groveling to please the powerful; hiding their real beliefs. A people with its own country could cure itself of those self-hatreds and self-doubts. A Jewish nation, they believed, would make the Jewish people strong.

But Jewish nationalists faced two problems: one with their fellow Jews, and the other with Ottomans who controlled Palestine. The Bible promises that Jews will return to their land when the Messiah, the redeemer, comes. Christians believe Jesus was that Messiah. Jews believe the Messiah is still to come. For strict, religious Jews, then, it was fine to wish to return to Israel. But when the exile should end was entirely up to God. The return of Jews to Israel was not a matter of human choice but of faith.

To this day, the land of Israel has two meanings for Jews. It is a nation like any other. But it is also a kind of moral ideal, a vision of Jews united, working to live according to the highest principles. For some those principles are religious laws, for others the ideals have been drawn from socialism, and for still others the guiding light is just a high ethical standard of being human.

From the 1800s on, Zionism was the expression of the Jewish yearning to have a state like any other, and Jews' wish to live more fulfilling and humane lives. That blend of two distinct dreams is very much like our story in the United States. In one way our history tells how thirteen colonies became a strong and feared nation. But in another sense our deepest belief is that Americans will be better human beings if they live in a vibrant, inclusive democracy.

In the nineteenth century, Jews listened as other peoples in Europe spoke of their determination to have their own nations. The Germans, the Italians, the Greeks were not waiting for God. They organized political parties, collected money, and trained fighters. Then Theodore Herzl, a Jewish journalist born in Vienna, made a bold suggestion: Jews did not have to wait any longer. Herzl wrote, "We are a *people, one* people. We have everywhere tried honestly to integrate with the national communities surrounding us and to retain only our faith. We are not permitted to do so." He was saying that Jews could be like any other ethnic group. They did not need God to lead them home. They could build a homeland for themselves.

Herzl was also warning Jews. His home city of Vienna—in which there were many prosperous, famous Jews—elected an openly anti-Semitic mayor. To Herzl this was the final straw, the proof. Not only *could* Jews have a homeland, they *must* have one.

Herzl was a realist. He did not need any signs from heaven to build a homeland for Jews. But that meant he came up against the problem of international politics. The Ottomans did not want to permit Jews to make Palestine their own. Herzl was open to other locations—maybe Argentina, out west in America, perhaps somewhere in Africa. The Jews, he thought, needed a land of their own, where, as a people, they could build a nation. Herzl was ready to debate and negotiate over which land that would be, but he knew that the homeland Jews longed for was in Palestine.

Would the Jews, the Arabs, the world have avoided decades of bloodshed if Herzl had settled on, say, Mozambique or Uganda instead of Palestine? I don't think so. Large groups of European newcomers filled with modern ideas and an ancient faith would have clashed with local peoples anywhere in the world. In fact, that is exactly what did happen to Christians when they arrived in South America after Columbus, in North America after Jamestown, and on and on in Australia, in Africa, and in Asia. Moreover, in the 1900s, Europeans would have made some effort to take over and modernize the Holy Land, with Christians if not Jews as settlers. The area meant so much to the Christians for historical and religious reasons (among others) that they would certainly have wanted to control and "improve" it. And that would have led to conflicts with the Palestinians already living there.

Herzl spoke of the Jews as a "people"—not of Judaism, the religion. Indeed, Zionism was bitterly opposed by the most devout Jews, who believed it was totally wrong for Herzl, or any human being, to bring Jews back to Israel. They were sure that only God, only the Messiah, could do that. So Zionism, the very force that built Israel as a Jewish state, was not a call for Jews to be observant, to abide by ancient laws, or even to be religious at all. Today, the distinction between Israel as a homeland for Jewish people, and Israel as a state in which the laws of the Jewish religion have a special place, has blurred. But that is a recent and troubling development that I will discuss later on. It is not what Herzl and the early Zionists had in mind.

The first wave of Jews to come to Palestine lasted from about 1882 to 1904. About twenty-five or thirty-five thousand settlers came to work on farms, and had a very hard time of it. Only support from the wealthy Baron Edmund James de Rothschild enabled them to survive.

My grandfather Solomon was not part of this very first wave of immigrants to Israel, but his story fits well enough. He was the chief rabbi of Kiev, which is now in Ukraine and was then part of Russia. Like all devout Jews of his time, he had a long beard, wore black, and believed deeply in Jewish law and traditions. But he also thought it important to be in touch with the modern world. He made sure his ten children learned Russian as well as Yiddish and Hebrew. And when one of the Jews in Kiev was arrested on the basis of a vicious falsehood called "the blood libel," he joined with other Jewish leaders to fight the issue in court.

The Fixer by Bernard Malamud is a wonderful novel about this

My grandfather, Rabbi Solomon Aronson. He brought the family out of Kiev to Palestine in the 1920s.

case. Menahim Beilis had been accused of killing a Christian boy to use his blood in a Jewish ceremony. The blood libel, the sick idea that Jews baked their Passover bread with the blood of Christian children, was invented in England in the 1200s, and was then passed around Europe, from country to country. Here it was, 1911, and the accusation came up again. My grandfather and other Jewish leaders went to court to defend Mr. Beilis. They brought in experts on Judaism, who proved to an all-Christian jury that the blood libel was a prejudice, a fantasy that had nothing to do with real Jews or real Judaism.

The fact that Beilis was acquitted showed that the light of reason was breaking in, just a bit, on the darkness of anti-Semitism. But my grandfather felt that a world in which Jews were so vulnerable was not the best place for him or his children. When he was invited to move to Tel Aviv to be one of the leading rabbis there, he accepted. That was what Zionism offered—an escape from a world of prejudice and hatred, an opportunity to build a flourishing new homeland.

The tragedy is that the more Jews who arrived in Palestine to build their Jewish homeland, the clearer it became to the Palestinians living there that they needed their own state too. Today, both Israelis and Palestinians are passionate nationalists. Indeed, ask Palestinians who know their history, and they will agree that their people learned their nationalism from the Jews. All want a nation for their own people, with their own culture and traditions, on the very same piece of land. And that intense nationalism is what makes Israel feel so alien to me. My own father chose the internationalism of New York. So I recoil when Israeli Jews tell me Arabs are of a different race, or Arabs say Jews should be pushed into the sea. That kind of nationalism is poisonous. And yet without such passionate nationalism, Israel would not exist.

WAR, INTRIGUES, AND DECLARATIONS

In 1913, most of the world was controlled by vast empires: the Russian tsars ruled from Siberia and the Pacific to the borders of Eastern Europe; the Hapsburg monarchs of the Austro-Hungarian Empire dominated Eastern and Central Europe; and the Ottoman Empire stretched from the edges of the Austro-Hungarian and Russian lands all the way around the Mediterranean, across the Holy Land, and through Egypt. The British Empire touched every continent, and was home to fully a quarter of the peoples in the world. Empires were the opposite of nationalist states: You belonged in an empire if you were in a land ruled by a tsar, sultan, emperor, or king. Your language, your culture, your faith, were swallowed up in that larger kingdom. Nationalists were determined to tear empires apart, and they succeeded.

World War I began in 1914 when an assassin, desperate to create an independent Serbia, murdered the crown prince of the Austro-Hungarian Empire. Throughout Europe—indeed, throughout the world—nationalists gave their lives to carve out their homelands as new nations. Croats, Armenians, Czechs, Slovaks, Poles, Lithuanians, Estonians, Latvians, Hungarians, Irish, Jews, Arabs, and Kurds all saw the cracking of empires as their golden moment, their chance to have nations of their own.

When President Wilson took America into the war, he promised that he was not just risking American lives to prop up foolish kings or cruel empires. He was actually fighting for the principle of the "self-determination of peoples." Wilson believed that when the war was over, people throughout the world would begin to taste the same freedoms as Americans. In fact, America had just begun its own overseas empire, taking over Cuba and the Philippines in 1898. But both

Wilson and average Americans really did believe they were fighting a war to make "the world . . . safe for democracy." They thought that creating many nations could solve the world's problems—especially the bloody problem of nationalism.

Here is where the story gets more complicated—where reasons of war and political calculation conflicted with those ideals of democracy and self-determination. In 1917 the British foreign secretary, Lord Balfour, wrote a letter to Lord Rothschild, which was later published as a short statement in the London *Times*. In what has become known as the Balfour Declaration, he said, "His Majesty's Government view with favour the establishment in Palestine of a national home for the Jewish people . . . it being clearly understood that nothing shall be done which may prejudice the civil and religious rights of existing non-Jewish communities in Palestine. . . ."

To Jews this was the most marvelous news. For the first time in two thousand years a strong power likely to control their ancient homeland was promising to help them return. Even fifty years after Balfour, when I was a student in Hebrew school, I remember the thrill that came with reading his words. I felt as though all of Jewish history were a tense, action-packed movie in which we barely escaped from destruction, and now, finally, I knew the good guys were coming. To be more precise, I felt like I was reading the Emancipation Proclamation. At last, the end of the darkness was in sight.

Of course, to a Palestinian, the Balfour Declaration was a sign that the darkness was descending.

The problem is that the declaration was issued amid the gunfire and slaughter of World War I. Government spokesmen say whatever suits their purposes during a war. Two years earlier another English official promised Arab leaders that if they broke away from the

Ottomans, the English would give them lands of their own. Although the extent of those lands was not clear, the Arabs believed they included Palestine. And the French, also looking for allies, were making their own bargains and promises involving Palestine at exactly the same time. The great powers were putting out bait, enticing Jews and Arabs to side with them during the war.

By the time the war had ended, the Ottomans had been overthrown and their empire was gone forever. The victors of World War I decided to carve up the Middle East as they saw fit. France was given authority over Syria and Lebanon. England took responsibility for what is now Israel and Jordan. Although this resolution may look harsh to our modern eyes, that is simply how winning and losing in war has worked throughout human history.

To give just one telling example: In the 1820s, when the Greeks fought to become an independent nation, the ruling Ottomans called on the Egyptians for support. The Egyptians invaded Greek lands, and their plan was for more than just a military conquest. According to the historian Paul Johnson, the invaders hoped to pay for the war by driving out Greek farmers and replacing them with Egyptians. Clearly, the Ottomans and Arabs of the 1820s did not see anything wrong with taking over a land, evicting its people, and making it their own.

But there was something different about this conquest, this war. Supposedly World War I was to end the age of empires and to usher in freedom, democracy, and "the self-determination of peoples." So the English and French announced that they were deeply concerned about fulfilling their "sacred trust" to advance the "well-being and development" of the people and places under their care. The Europeans created a new kind of status, a "mandate." A mandate is like a child given temporary foster care; it is a land ruled for the moment by a more advanced country, only until it is ready for self government.

England and France did not claim they were grabbing the old Ottoman lands, the way straightforward conquerors have always done. Instead they were merely being wise and kind helpers, carefully tending to the betterment of their charges until the peoples in those regions could stand on their own. In reality, the Europeans were all calculating how to dominate the Middle East while officially preparing to withdraw. They had many good reasons to care about the region: Christian Europeans all wanted access to those holy sites. The British felt it was crucial to have friendly powers near the Suez Canal in Egypt since so much of their shipping passed through it. And then there was oil.

World War I could really be called the victory of oil over coal and hay. The British converted their powerful navy from coal-burning ships to oil-burning ones just before the war, in 1912. Two years later, in order to guarantee that it would have enough oil to power those ships, the British government made a long-term deal with a company that was just starting to drill oil wells in what is now Iran. When the war began, most armies moved on coal-fueled railroads and ships, and on horses. During the war, armies switched to using recently invented cars, trucks, motorcycles, tanks, airplanes, and oil-burning ships. Ten days after the war ended, Lord Curzon of England explained that the Allies had won the war by floating "to victory upon a wave of oil." Seeing how important oil would be in the future, Lord Balfour— whose declaration meant so much to Jews—was more explicit about England's aims for the Middle East: "I do not care under what system we keep the oil, but I am quite clear it is all-important for us that this oil should be available." While there is no oil in what is now Israel, the

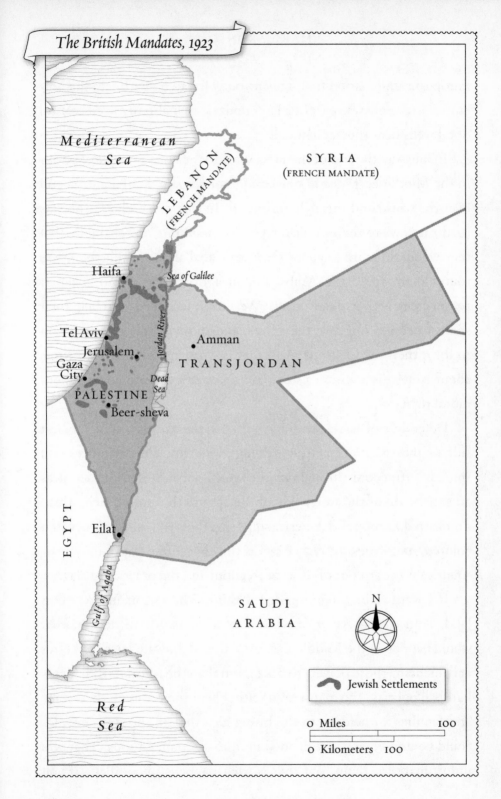

The British Mandates, 1923

Mediterranean Sea

LEBANON (FRENCH MANDATE)

SYRIA (FRENCH MANDATE)

Haifa

Sea of Galilee

Tel Aviv

Jerusalem

Gaza City

Jordan River

PALESTINE

Dead Sea

Beer-sheva

Amman

TRANSJORDAN

EGYPT

Eilat

Gulf of Aqaba

SAUDI ARABIA

N

Red Sea

Jewish Settlements

0 Miles 100

0 Kilometers 100

Europeans understood that figuring out what to do with, say, the holy city of Jerusalem was part of a larger puzzle that also involved control of oil wells near the Persian Gulf.

In one way, the end of the First World War saw a transfer of power in the Middle East, just as one conqueror has supplanted another all over the world and throughout history. In that sense, the Europeans used the Jews to serve their own ends—assuming, for example, that they would do more to guard the Suez Canal and thus valuable trade routes than would the Arabs. But in another way the transfer of power came with two new ideals: Western rulers needed to help their subject peoples improve their lives, and those people had the right to form their own nations. And that is what makes it hard to think about Israel—it is always a story half about raw power and half about moral right.

Defenders of Israel see the country as the expression of the best side of the twentieth century: doing away with old prejudices and spreading freedom throughout the world. Critics of Israel see it as an expression of the worst side of the twentieth century: rich, white-dominated Europe and America imposing their will on helpless, often colored, minorities. In fact, Israel is the child of both trends, just as America was born out of ideas of freedom and the practice of slavery.

If I want to be tough minded, I think: The Ottomans lost; England, France, and America won. The winners got to decide what would happen in the Middle East. And they did. If the Jews did better at convincing those powers to back them than the Muslims did, that is hardball politics. Too many Arabs either kept their eyes on their clans and families, or held on to the losing idea that all the Arab peoples could be unified and not divided up into separate nations. That was unfortunate for them. But that is what happens in conflicts: If you back the wrong horse, you lose. The Arabs may feel frustrated, resentful, even furious about that outcome. But that anger does nothing to change political facts.

And yet even from a pro-Israeli point of view this is not a very comforting argument. There are Muslims who insist that the world has changed. The West needs oil and an end to terrorist threats more than it needs Israel. If the Jews were the hardball winners after World War I, why can't the Muslims be the hardball winners ninety years later?

We can now begin to answer that first question, Why is Israel so hated? Israel loses both ways. If you resent the fact that Europeans decided the fate of the Middle East, you feel Balfour was wrong in 1917 and the Jews never should have been encouraged to find a national home in the area. If you believe winners are free to do as they like, you wonder why the oil-rich Arabs don't get to shape the region's fate today.

I sometimes think that Israel is a kind of younger sibling, or cousin, of America. It is passing through a history similar to ours, but on a much smaller scale and delayed by a few centuries. The British started settling in North America in 1607, whereas Jews began to heed Herzl's call in the 1880s. No wonder, then, that Israel feels both familiar and alien. And yet, from Herzl on, moving to America and building Israel were opposite choices. Jews needed to decide which one truly was a "national home for the Jewish people." The similarity and dissimilarity of Israel and America lead to my next question: Where should the home of the Jewish people be?

WHERE SHOULD A "NATIONAL HOME FOR THE JEWISH PEOPLE" BE?

Modern Israel is a country built by immigrants, much like modern America. Of course, the immigrants to Israel are mainly Jewish, while those coming to America are from every background; but as Israelis discovered, the differences between, say, highly educated, antireligious, German Jews and almost tribal, deeply religious Middle Eastern Jews are extreme. It was no easier for Israel to accept so many different types of people into a very small country than it was for America to take many more peoples into a very large one.

Israelis define their history by the various waves of immigrants who came after Herzl. But they use a special term: not "wave," as if immigrants were a kind of tide, but "aliyah"—"rising, ascent." The idea is that to come to Israel is uplifting, unlike merely shifting from one place to another. Moving to Israel is a kind of pilgrimage. Although that may sound like a religious belief, it is actually pure nationalism: the idea that a Jew can only find him- or herself in the Jewish land. (In the 1960s some African Americans came to feel the same way about Africa, and moved to, for example, Tanzania.) It is that very concept— that Jews need to be in Israel to flourish—that I find most troubling. And that idea has divided Jews ever since Herzl.

Zionists have always insisted that building Israel is the only right choice for a Jew. But from the first aliyah on, most Jews have not accepted that argument. For example, when that first group of some twenty-five to thirty-five thousand Jews moved to Palestine to build the Zionist dream, some four hundred and fifty thousand Jews moved to America from Russia alone. And there was even a third choice. A large faction of European Jews rejected both Zionism and immigration. They believed the hope of the future lay in socialism. Workers of the world, they thought, were united by their economic challenges. Religion, nation, traditions—all of these were secondary to the fight of workers for their rights. These socialists were the opposite of nationalists. They wanted to erase borders between peoples, not built new ones.

Clearly Zionism was not *the* choice for Jews; it was *a* choice for Jews. Still, it spoke to the deepest feelings of many European Jews. The next wave of immigration, from 1904 to 1914, the second aliyah, brought some forty thousand more Jews to Palestine. This second "rising" was interrupted by World War I and picked up again from 1919 to 1923, when another forty thousand arrived in Palestine.

My cousin Dov was one of those Zionist pioneers who left Europe in the 1920s and moved to build a farm on the brown hills of Galilee. Neither he nor any of his friends or family were religious. They were devoted to building a farm, plowing the soil, growing a community. Their God was in work and in shared effort, not in prayer or the holy books. Those early Zionists remind me of the sodbusters in Nebraska: Even in faded black-and-white pictures, you can see how hard their life was. There is the tall awkward Dov, with his thick glasses, determined to be a farmer.

Dov always used to laugh about psychological problems. Just go out and work in the soil, he would say, that will cure you. People like Dov believed that tough physical work made you into a better person. He had no doubt that he had made the right choice in moving to Palestine and living on a kibbutz, a collective farm.

If you want to know how Israel is different from America, the kibbutz is one place to start. While America's history is built around the stories of individuals striking out on their own by going west to

This photo, taken in 1937, shows what Israel meant to the early Zionists: weak Jews of the European ghetto, who spent all day praying, being transformed into strong men who worked the land.

make their fortunes, the kibbutz was, for the longest time, the very symbol of Zionism: the best, the truest expression, of modern Israel.

THE KIBBUTZ: HERRING IN THE GALILEE

A kibbutz is the very opposite of the American story of a family hitching up a wagon and heading out to homestead their own piece of land. Kibbutzim (the plural of "kibbutz") are collective farms where the land, homes, tractors, and livestock are owned by the group, not by any individual. Children did not even live with their parents most of the time; instead they were reared together in a special children's dorm and visited their families when there was room in their schedules. Everyone was to work together for the common good, to discuss and vote on how to spend money, and to provide for everyone's needs.

In America, people own cars as soon as they can. Even when cars became popular and easily available in Israel, no one on a kibbutz owned a car. The kibbutz had cars that you could only use by making a formal request and demonstrating a special need. In other words, the kibbutzim were socialist, not capitalist. The good of the group, decided by the group, came first; not the rights of the individual.

In Dov's time, the kibbutzim ranged from mildly to extremely antireligious. Jews went to a kibbutz to leave behind everything associated with their lives in Europe. They cut off their beards, took off their black robes, put down their religious books, and picked up socialist tracts or pamphlets on crop rotation. According to one story I've read, a group of early Zionists celebrated Yom Kippur, the most holy day in the Jewish year, by eating ham sandwiches right in front of the Wailing Wall in Jerusalem. Since devout Jews pray at the wall, are supposed to fast on Yom Kippur, and are not allowed to eat any kind of pork at any time, the Zionists were breaking every religious commandment at once—which was precisely their point.

The kibbutz stood for the idea that a national home for Jews means a place in which individual Jews find their strength from working the land together with other Jews, with religion left out of the matter. America stood for the idea that a national home for Jews means a large nation where Jews are a minority, but individual Jews are free to follow any occupation and to have any belief. One vision puts the group first, the other centers on the individual, as I discovered when I went to stay with Dov.

The essence of the kibbutz was the dining room, where everyone ate together. When I spent one summer on Alonim, Dov's kibbutz, in the 1960s, we all sat at long tables, as in a huge school lunchroom. At breakfast time there were bowls on the table with vegetables— tomatoes, cucumber, onions grown on the farm—hearty vegetables, not sweet fruits. The pears we picked were to be sold. Our fruit came in a cold soup made up out of the plums, apples, and pears that were bruised and could not be marketed. Then gray metal carts came around, offering two or three kinds of yogurt, salty herring, and eggs. No American cereals.

A couple of years later I'd be at Brandeis, a primarily Jewish university in America. Often enough, we had bagels, French toast, and pancakes at breakfast. When we took over a building as part of an anti–Vietnam War protest, the Jewish mothers served us potato pancakes with apple sauce, and the really cool hippies brought in huge bags of crunchy nuts and grains combined in what they called "granola." Those were the Jewish foods I knew. So being at the

My cousin Dov and his family lived in this kibbutz, Alonim. Taken in 1938, this shows the ideal of the kibbutz: everyone pitching in to do what was necessary to create, defend, and improve the collective farm. Today, Alonim earns much of its income from a McDonald's franchise, which is the last thing any of these pioneers could have imagined.

kibbutz was strange. Here we were in the hills of Galilee, down the road from Nazareth, eating yogurt, herring, cheese—the foods of northern Europe. Breakfast looked back to Europe, and was good for you. It was not a time for sweets. This was socialism: the group together, doing what was right. If someone had snuck in a bag of corn-flakes, he would have been seen as a traitor.

The kibbutzim were a perfect combination of idealism and prag-matism. They were idealistic because every man, woman, and child was working to build a better future for all. To this day, older Israelis who grew up on kibbutzim still have that shine, that fire. They were shaped by a world where working together for all was more important than trying to "make it" on their own. The kibbutzim were also prac-tical. They were a way for Jews to band together, work hard, protect one another, and establish themselves in Palestine. They were instant communities—and instant forts.

At first, some kibbutzim hired local Arabs to work for them. But by the 1920s, the kibbutzim had shifted. They decided that they should be entirely Jewish, with Jews doing everything from cleaning the chicken coops to washing mounds of diapers. The kibbutzim were an expression of absolute determination. Even Jews who had never seen a single cow would become farmers. They would give up all their possessions; let others decide what jobs they should do; work from dawn to darkness. They would give every ounce of themselves. And they would build settlements that could last.

Most Jews who moved to Israel found this too hard, or not to their liking. At the very most some 15 percent of Jews in Palestine became kibbutzniks, but in most years the percentage was much lower. The Israeli historian Tom Segev points out that Jews created the bus-tling city of Tel Aviv at the very same time they established the first kibbutzim. Tel Aviv was much more like what Israel would become than were the collective farms. But the kibbutz, the group working together as pioneers to build Israel, came to stand for the essence of the country. In America, almost all of our schoolbooks make a similar choice in looking back to colonial days. Every textbook speaks about New England town meetings and Virginia plantations. But, in fact, business-minded cities such as New York or Philadelphia were much more like what America would later become.

Were the kibbutzim really idealistic, you might ask, if they did not work with their Arab neighbors? One answer lies in the nature of socialism. Socialists felt that their view of the world was rational and modern. They saw capitalism—a system in which everyone is in a mad scramble to make the most for him- or herself—as wasteful and destructive. To socialists, capitalism was a lingering holdover from the nineteenth century, destined to collapse under its own weight. Socialism was the rational choice, the path to the future. If the kibbutzniks saw capitalism as outdated, they viewed the lives of the nearby Muslims as positively medieval.

To the kibbutzniks, Muslims seemed like relics from another century. They belonged to clans whose leaders had great power, they kept sheep and donkeys, not tractors and trucks; they believed in many superstitions, and were allowed to have more than one wife. The kibbutzniks were not judging Islam, the religion of the Muslims— they didn't have any sympathy for Jews wasting their days in prayer either. Instead, the kibbutzniks viewed their Muslim neighbors as primitives who needed to be educated.

The journalist Jeffrey Goldberg recalls growing up in the late 1970s on Long Island and reading about Israel in a Reform Jewish Hebrew school. His book passed along the kibbutzniks' beliefs about Arabs as if they were facts: "side by side with the Jews lived the Arabs. . . . Most of them were farmers, working on backward farms and living in primitive villages. . . . The Arab farmers saw the fertile Jewish farms and the rapidly growing settlements. . . . 'See!' said the Jewish farmers. 'There is a better way to live.'"

Had Muslims come, hat in hand, and said, "Teach us, show us how to be modern, how to live the new life of socialism, reason, and science," the Jews would have been pleased. But, realistically, the Arabs were never going to do that.

First, people like Dov built a tower, then a few corrugated metal huts, then they planted fields, tilled by tractors and patrolled with guns. And in their nearby villages, tending their olive trees and orchards, the Arabs could see new people coming and the land changing. In hard times, some Arab farmers had been forced to sell their land to rich Muslim landlords. The absentee owners were happy to sell off those fields to the Jews, who were willing to pay the highest prices. So the Jews bought land and built their kibbutzim, while their Muslim neighbors felt threatened and grew angry.

THE AMERICAN PARALLEL

The Muslims who saw Jews arriving and changing the land did not agree with the whole idea of a mandate. They made that clear at a meeting in 1920 where they insisted that Palestine (a British mandate) and Syria (a French mandate) were still united. And they were absolutely opposed to the Zionists. "Boycott the Jews," Arabs were urged, "sell them nothing and buy nothing from them."

Looking back, we can see that the Muslim position was guaranteed to lose. But that is only clear in retrospect. The Arabs were in a difficult position after World War I. The rules they understood had suddenly changed. Throughout history, groups have been in similar positions: a proud people, with set ways, have lived on the land for centuries. Then an armed newcomer shows up and tells them they must obey new rules. There are no good choices under those conditions.

Take the Indians in the American Northeast shortly before the American Revolution. All they could see were greedy American settlers eager to buy or steal their land. That is how Muslims saw the arriving Jews. In 1763, Neolin, an Indian prophet, began preaching that if Indians stopped using the settlers' goods, the invaders would disappear. Again, that is just like the boycott the Arabs tried in 1920. Everywhere Neolin went, Indians took up arms. A great rebellion led by Pontiac broke out. And it nearly succeeded—until the Indians ran out of ammunition. Something similar happened in Palestine.

In 1935 a Muslim preacher named Izz al-Din al-Qassam was inspired to fight, by news that the Zionists were collecting large numbers of guns. It was not long before he was killed, but first his voice, then his death, sparked what has been called the Great Revolt. Exactly as in Pontiac's Rebellion, the Muslims tried to stop the encroachments of settlers and to drive out the occupying power whose authority they did not accept. It took the English the better part of two years, but they crushed the revolt.

In 1937, after seeing the rage of the Great Revolt, the English asked a high official to report on conditions in the mandate. Earl Peel suggested dividing up Palestine, giving some to the Jews, most to the Muslims, and retaining key holy sites under English control. Peel's suggestion had no chance since Muslims rejected the entire idea of splitting up Palestine, and the Jews were demanding ever more land. So the English decided to start all over again. In 1939 the English issued a White Paper announcing that once Jews and Muslims found a way to work together, a new state would be created. It would be dominated by the Arabs, who would have two thirds of the population, but the Jews would have some voice of their own. Until then, the sale of land to Jews would be controlled by the British, and Jewish immigration over the next five years would be limited to a total of seventy-five thousand people.

The Peel plan of dividing Palestine into two states is what, I am sure, will eventually happen—although not within the White Paper's borders. There will be an Israel and a Palestine, with some clever solution for Jerusalem. The 1939 White Paper, though, is what idealists wish could have happened: Jews and Palestinians together creating a mini-America, a shared state with rights for all. And, in fact, if you spend enough time with Israeli Jewish young people who eat Arab foods, enjoy Arab music, and who look physically very similar to Arabs, you can just picture what a joint Jewish–Arab Middle Eastern nation might have been. But to get a sense of just how unrealistic that dream was in 1939, just look at American history.

Back in the 1760s, the English felt some sympathy for the Indians who were losing their land. They also had no desire to spend more money, and send more soldiers, to protect annoying colonists and to fight off angry Indians. So in 1763 they decreed that Americans could not settle the lands west of the Alleghenies. That was a nice idea. But England was not willing to do much of anything to make the so-called Proclamation Line work.

The 1939 White Paper was very much like the 1763 Proclamation Line: No matter how good each plan looked on paper, neither had a chance without a total commitment from the English. London did not have the will, the funds, or the wherewithal to turn either idealistic dream into a reality. Instead, once the Americans won the Revolution, they streamed into Indian lands; and even as the 1939 White Paper was being circulated, the Jews and the Palestinians each grew tougher, stronger, and more determined than ever to have their own nations, ruled their own ways, in the ancient Holy Land.

Although kibbutzniks like Dov were well aware of the rising anger of nearby Muslims, they had no doubts. They were certain that building a community that could feed itself with its own crops and protect itself with its own guns was the best hope—indeed, the only hope—for Jews. A homeland for Jews had to be a place under Jewish control, defended with Jewish bullets.

Was that true? Until the mid-1920s, most Jews did not think so. Instead, the overwhelming majority of those who chose to leave their homes headed off to America.

WHERE CAN JEWS FIND SAFETY?

Between 1890 and 1924 some two million Jews chose to move to America. By contrast, in 1923, there were perhaps ninety thousand Jews in Palestine. Clearly, America was the new homeland for Jews. But only so long as the Jews could adjust and blend in to America. It was the same for the millions of desperately poor Italians: They were welcome in to the United States so long as they did not remain too Italian. In the 1920s more and more Americans became convinced that neither the Jews nor the Italians ever really could become good citizens. They were just too different. Membership in the Ku Klux

Klan reached all time highs in the 1920s, as the Klan added the cause of preventing immigration to its traditional aims of segregating and intimidating blacks. In 1924, Congress passed, and President Coolidge signed, laws designed to cut off the influx of Italians and Jews, so that America would become ever more white and Protestant.

America's restrictive immigration law created the fourth aliyah. Between 1924 and 1929 some eighty-two thousand Europeans moved to Palestine, nearly doubling the Jewish population. Most of those immigrants, who generally hailed from large cities in Poland, would have gone to America if they could. They stayed in the growing city of Tel Aviv, and set up their own small businesses, showing no interest in the socialism of the kibbutzim. They felt comfortable in an urban business center, not on a dusty collective farm. In fact, some twenty-three thousand of them were so unhappy they went on to leave Palestine.

America's turn toward exclusion did more than swell the numbers of Jews in Palestine: It fed the Zionist argument. If the land of the Statue of Liberty could close its doors to Jews, that seemed to prove that Jews could never be safe in a place where they were a minority. How safe could Jews be in a nation so ready to pass anti-Semitic laws? And not just pass laws. Leo Frank, an innocent Jew accused of raping and murdering a white girl, was lynched in Georgia in 1915, before a cheering crowd. In the 1920s, Henry Ford, father of the American automobile industry, insisted that dealers who sold his cars subscribe to the *Dearborn Independent*, a newspaper he owned. Ford filled the paper with the most anti-Semitic articles, including fraudulent allegations of a Jewish conspiracy to rule the world. In 1938, Ford held a giant dinner, at which he proudly accepted an award of distinction granted to him by Adolf Hitler's Nazi government.

Ford was hardly alone in his extreme anti-Semitism. In the 1930s a Catholic priest named Father Charles Coughlin built up a radio audience of twenty million Americans. At first he spoke as the working-man's friend, arguing for laws guaranteeing that all Americans would be well paid. But then he shifted into attacking Jews. Not only did his followers urge that Jews escaping from Hitler be sent back to Europe "in leaky boats," but they gathered guns in a plot to kill important Jews in America. To Zionists, the rise of Hitler in Germany and the open anti-Semitism in the United States were proof positive: Only a Jewish homeland could offer true sanctuary to Jews.

THE HOLOCAUST

Hitler was elected chancellor of Germany in 1933, and as conditions worsened in Europe, Jews fled to Palestine. Indeed, some two hundred thousand Jews made it to Palestine in the 1930s, which more than doubled the Jewish population. But the strict British limits on new Jewish immigration took effect in 1939, just as World War II began. By now the British clearly needed Arab oil, and they were dead set against stirring up trouble in Palestine by allowing in more Jews. When boats arrived carrying desperate Jews, they were turned away. Some boats even sank, taking six hundred lives. Under the stern British eye, only about fourteen thousand Jews made it to safety in Palestine during each year of the war.

Americans were equally determined to make sure the United States would not be a haven for Jews escaping from Nazi Germany. Hitler's plan to unite Germany by treating Jews as subhuman pariahs was explicitly spelled out in his writings, which anyone could read, and the Nazis put his ideas into practice. By November 1938, when the Nazis went on a rampage of destruction against Jews, no one could doubt that Jews needed to leave the country. Yet attitudes in America did not change. In 1939, when the *St. Louis*, a boat carrying nine hundred European Jews, was refused entry in Cuba, it sailed to Miami. Although the boat was in sight of America, popular sentiment was strongly against letting the passengers into the country, since it would mean slightly expanding the quota for Jews. The boat was turned away and many of the Jews on it later perished in the Holocaust. In fact, the American officials processing Jewish applications in this period were so anti-Semitic that the tiny quotas set for Jews were often not filled.

By January 1942 the Nazis decided that brutalizing and murdering some Jews was not enough. Now they set about to create a "final solution" to the "Jewish problem" by systematically killing off all Jews in their infamous concentration camps. Yet even a 1943 proposal to allow twenty thousand Jewish children to be saved by coming to America was rejected by the State Department. While President Roosevelt knew, for certain, about the cattle cars filled with doomed people and the machinery of the death camps, he also knew that his only chance of ending this unspeakable crime was to bring America into the war without making it a war over the Jews. Of all the nations of the world, only Denmark and Bulgaria devoted themselves to protecting their Jews, and only one city, Shanghai, allowed every Jew who made it there to enter and find shelter.

The bland compliance of the Nazi clerks, carefully checking off Jewish names; the anti-Semitism of Europeans throughout the continent, who turned in or refused to harbor their Jewish neighbors; the brutality of SS soldiers specially assigned to round up and murder Jews; the efficiency of those visions of hell, the death camps, where humans were beaten and starved into skeletons, the still-living wraiths were poisoned with gas, and the corpses were fed into ovens to be reduced to heaps of bone and ash; the strict surveillance practiced by the British in Palestine; the tight quotas set by Americans; and the indifference of almost the entire world robbed six million individual Jewish boys and girls, teenagers, fathers and mothers, and elders of their lives.

We use the term "holocaust" so often that we forget what it means: extermination, complete destruction. The horror of the murders is disguised because six million is a number too large to comprehend and too familiar to penetrate. Think of it this way: It could only have happened because so many people wanted it to, or didn't mind, or looked the other way. The Holocaust was like the lynchings of blacks that were so popular in the American South—festive events at which thousands of people, families and even mothers with their young children—came to watch torture and murder. But here the lynching was of an entire people, and the enablers and bystanders were the entire world.

One essential answer to the question, How did Israel come to be? is, Because of the Holocaust. The Holocaust was the sum of all of the massacres, blood libels, pogroms, discriminatory immigration laws, and quotas that had previously convinced Zionists that they needed a homeland of their own. The death camps convinced those outside Israel of what the Zionists already believed: A world that could produce an Auschwitz must have an Israel.

Arguments about Israel quickly turn ferocious in good part because they are really about the Holocaust. Israel is not merely a country, but it represents the idea of sanctuary, of refuge; it stands for the conviction that Jews must be protected, must never again have to face extermination. Every baby born in Israel, every garden planted, every soldier parading behind the Israeli flag is an assertion: We did survive, we took your worst, we are alive and flourishing, while your Nazi regime was crushed into dust. To stand for Israel is to stand against Hitler. When I am in Israel I feel exactly that pride, and that impulse to spit on the grave of the Nazis. But strong feelings like that can blind you.

Israel is not just an expression of Jewish pride and of the Nazis' defeat. It is also a real place where people are as flawed and complex as anywhere else on the planet. To help to build Israel means to understand it as it is, not only for what it represents. The clearest way to see that is by looking at what the Holocaust meant to the Jews of Palestine while it was taking place. The view that many Zionists took of the frightened European Jews who managed to reach Palestine was not what a modern reader might expect.

Zionists have always been in competition with those who said Jews should move to America, or should pray, or should join the world alliance of socialists. As news of Hitler's crimes reached Palestine, many Zionists saw the suffering of the European Jews as proof that building a Jewish state had been the right choice all along. They viewed the Jews who were attacked, forced to wear stars, herded into ghettos and camps, as weak. Those defeated Jews were everything the Zionists had rejected and overcome by being pioneers in Palestine.

Miriam Groag, the mother of a cousin of mine, arrived in Palestine just after the war, ailing not only from having been in a concentration camp for three years, but having given birth in secret there. Having a baby was not only terribly difficult in a camp; it was forbidden. But a sympathetic guard protected her and her baby. Her husband, Willie, was a trained chemist, and they settled in a kibbutz founded by Jews

Miriam Groag, a cousin by marriage. She survived Terezin and even managed to give birth there, but was very weak and died from polio while living in Israel.

who shared their socialist outlook, and who came from the same part of Czechoslovakia as they did. But the kibbutzniks were not at all sympathetic to Marie's weakened condition. They saw her frailty and illness as her own failure. Miriam's daughter, Eve, survived not only the camp but the polio epidemic that eventually took her mother's life. Eve still remembers the harsh views of her Zionist neighbors. In their minds, living in Palestine on a kibbutz made Jews strong. If a person had resisted that truth and foolishly remained in Europe, her suffering was her fault.

Many Zionists of this period were extremely tough, determined people. They were hard Jews who scraped the stony hillsides to build settlements. They believed they had little or nothing in common with the weak, hapless, European Jews of the death camps. This may sound terribly cold, but it does give a sense of the pioneer mood of some of the Jews of Palestine. Like my cousin Dov, they literally believed they were creating a new kind of Jew by leaving Europe to work on the soil, and by building a land of their own. At the time of the American Revolution, Founding Fathers such as Thomas Jefferson held exactly the same belief. They were sure that the American farmer working his own plot of land was becoming a new kind of person who simply could not exist in the corrupt cities of Europe. The challenge of being a pioneer toughens people. Think of the homesteaders in places like Oklahoma, Nebraska, and Utah, where it took everything out of them just to survive. They had little room for soft feelings.

Zionists in Israel were Jewish, but, in their own minds, they were completely different from most other Jews. Still, there were those in Palestine who would do anything to help the suffering Jews of Europe. The most militant Jews were organizing terrorist cells to attack the British and drive them away so that the laws limiting

Jewish immigration would end, and Jews could take over the land. But the majority of Jews were willing to work with the British against Hitler. In fact, more than one hundred thousand Jews tried to join the British army to help out in the war effort. Some volunteered for the most dangerous missions: parachuting behind enemy lines in Europe to organize resistance against the Nazis. The most famous of these heroes was Hannah Szenes (pronounced "SEN-esh"), a Hungarian who had immigrated to Palestine. In 1944 she undertook a mission that brought her back to Hungary. She was captured, tortured, and executed. Hannah was twenty-three when she was killed. To this day, her poetry gives a sense of what an intense person she was:

> *Blessed is the match that burned and kindled flames,*
> *Blessed is the flame that set hearts on fire.*
> *Blessed are the hearts that knew how to die with honor,*
> *Blessed is the match that burned and kindled flames.*

The question of how the Jews of Palestine responded to the Holocaust while it was taking place, of whether to emphasize their heartless attitudes (Miriam Groag's story was not at all unusual) or their heroic efforts is still being debated to this day. But what of its broader meaning? What message did the death camps send to all Jews everywhere?

As late as the 1960s and '70s, my Israeli relatives were still taking seriously the idea that "it" could happen in America. America, they warned me, could turn into another Germany: a sophisticated, cultured nation that becomes a death chamber for Jews. Germany was the most modern nation in the world, they told me. It had the best universities, the smartest professors. Jews fooled themselves into believing they could blend in there, just as you American Jews are fooling yourselves about American tolerance; blending in never works.

That belief is the essence of nationalism: You need your own nation to be your own self. The Zionist version of nationalism is: Only in Israel can Jews ever, truly, be safe. That is an argument I have never believed.

Today it seems silly to imagine America turning into Nazi Germany. We did build camps to imprison Japanese Americans during World War II, but that was half a century ago, during a war, and those were not death factories. And my relatives were not only talking about the actual chances of a raving anti-Semite being elected president and setting up camps to murder Jews. Instead they were saying that a minority can never trust a majority to protect it. The minority needs its own place.

America is built around the opposite idea: As we all compete with one another, we find the common good together. That is a fundamental difference between Israeli Jews and American Jews. Israelis find strength by being in their own nation; Americans find strength by being in a nation in which they can compete as equals with everyone else.

Where is the homeland for Jews? The answer in the first half of the twentieth century was: It depended on which kind of person you were—whether you were more drawn to be part of a group and settled on ancient land, or if you were eager to make it on your own and happy to live in a modern, international city; if you were fortunate enough to be let into America, or if you were locked out of its doors. As ever with us Jews, one question had many answers—and those would keep changing even after the state of Israel was born.

What of the meaning of the Holocaust for non-Jews? The Holocaust is the pivot point; before that, anti-Semitism was acceptable, even popular. After the world saw the camps, not only did prejudice against Jews sour in the mouths of those who expressed it, but the rights of all minorities, all oppressed peoples gained new importance. And in that light, not only is the Holocaust the reason for Israel, but it poses the greatest moral challenge to Jewish Israelis. For the question they must answer is, Why, in a nation meant to be a haven for the persecuted of the Earth, did the Palestinians lose their land?

WHY DID THE PALESTINIANS LOSE THEIR LAND?

Anti-Zionists—Muslims, Arabs, Palestinians, critics of Israel—have all heard the story of the Holocaust. They know what Europeans did to the Jews and that America shut its doors. But, they say, why is that our problem? If America and Europe were inhuman to Jews, let America and Europe take care of them. Why should Muslims living in the Middle East have to suffer for the crimes of Christians thousands of miles away?

That argument simply ignores global realities, just as the Muslims in 1920 did not accept the division of the old Ottoman lands into English and French zones, and the Palestinians in 1937 rejected the Peel Commission. The winners of World War I, the rulers of the Middle East, were part of a world system. And the peoples of Palestine—Muslims, Christians, and Jews—had been linked economically to world markets, at least since the nineteenth century. Jews facing extermination in Europe and shut out of America were desperate to reach Palestine. That was a fact of human needs in an interconnected world. Similarly, in the 1760s, people from England were going to immigrate to America and seek to settle west of the Alleghenies. That, too, was an unchangeable fact.

But then, Palestinians say, what about the desperation of our families who lost their land when Israel was born? That is a crucial question. In a private memoir, Sari Nusseibeh's father, Anwar, wrote eloquently about the fate of his countrymen and their lost homes: "Acre, Nazaraeth, Safad, Ramle, Lydda, and all the other towns and villages of Palestine mean more than red dots on the map. They mean the warm hearths and proud homes of an old established community. The hearths have turned to ashes and homes ground to dust and the life that once throbbed within them throbs no more."

What happened during Israel's War of Independence in 1948, which resulted in the mass exodus of Palestinians? If the Holocaust is the proof that Israel must exist, the fate of the Palestinians when the state of Israel was born is the soul-searching question Israeli Jews must answer.

By 1946 the British were exhausted. They had just fought their second horrific world war. London itself was gray, its buildings coated with soot, or smashed by German rockets and bombs. The British people were battered, the nation was in debt, and all around the world the British faced nothing but trouble. In India, the "crown jewel" of the British Empire, the people could not wait to throw their rulers out. And to make the exit of the British more complicated, the Muslims of India insisted on having a country of their own.

Then there was Palestine. The English tried to manage the relentless Jews and angry Arabs of the mandate. But in July of 1946, the most extreme faction of Jewish terrorists blew up the British headquarters at the King David Hotel, killing ninety-one people. The

Jews were not willing to wait for England to decide what to do with Palestine; they chose to go ahead, on their own, and fight for it.

The British had had enough of trying to manage a world empire. In 1947, Britain turned the whole Palestine problem over to the United Nations, and, by August, agreed to let India be independent. Four nations were born out of those decisions: India, Pakistan, Israel, and Jordan. Bangladesh later broke off from Pakistan, and a Palestinian state may well take shape one day. That would mean that the departure of the British eventually led to the creation of six nations (or even seven, if Gaza and the West Bank split into two states). But to create those nations, millions upon millions of people left, fled, or were forced to run away from their homes. Hundreds of thousands of people were killed. Was all of that misery and bloodshed necessary?

Most of the deaths came when British India was partitioned into India and Pakistan. Some seven millions Muslims left India to move to Pakistan, passing some seven million Hindus who left what was about to become Pakistan to move to India. "Left" is far too mild a word: Desperate people fled, terrified people ran, frightened people escaped. Some moved because they wanted to, others because of the assaults on their communities convinced them that they needed to go. In the chaos and conflict, between two hundred thousand and one million people were killed. Since then, India and Pakistan have fought three wars. Both nations are now armed with nuclear weapons, which would make a fourth war almost too deadly to imagine. Nonetheless, Muslims who once lived in India have a nation of their own.

That is not how the departure of the British worked out in Palestine. At the end of 1947, the United Nations took over control of Palestine from England. After much struggle, UN officials came up with the idea of splitting up the state between Jews and Arabs, while

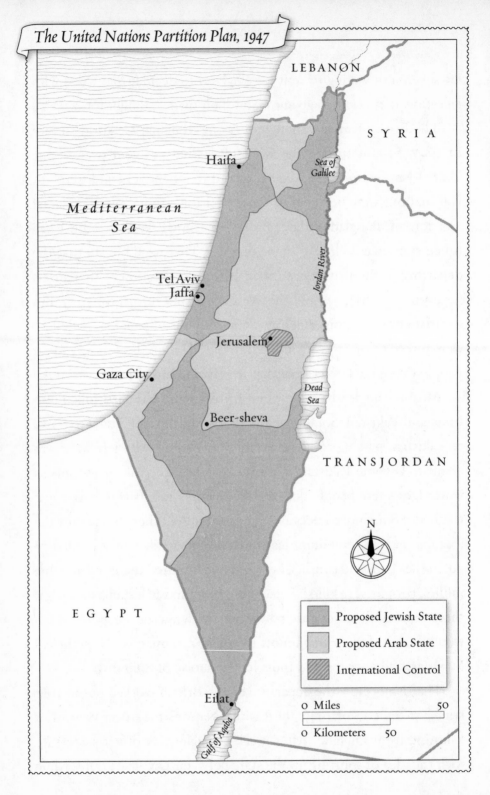

The United Nations Partition Plan, 1947

LEBANON

SYRIA

Mediterranean
Sea

Haifa

Sea of
Galilee

Jordan River

Tel Aviv
Jaffa

Jerusalem

Gaza City

Dead
Sea

Beer-sheva

TRANSJORDAN

N

EGYPT

Proposed Jewish State

Proposed Arab State

International Control

0   Miles   50

0   Kilometers   50

Eilat

Gulf of Aqaba

leaving Jerusalem under international control—an updated version of the 1937 Peel Plan. At the time, there were more than twice as many Muslims as Jews in Palestine: 1.4 million as compared to six hundred thousand. If you look within the borders of what would become Israel, there were about 870,000 Palestinians.

Jews and Arabs began fighting at once. On May 15 the following spring, the state of Israel was founded, and quickly recognized by the United States and the Soviet Union. In response, Muslim armies from Egypt, Syria, Iraq, and Saudi Arabia attacked. Their goal was to get rid of the Jews entirely. Jordan also fought against the Jews in Jerusalem, but otherwise held back. The fighting finally ended in 1949 when Israel and the Arabs agreed to a truce.

Not only did the Jews manage to fend off the Arab armies, they carved out more territory for themselves. The 1947 UN plan allocated them about 56 percent of the British Mandate, while the truce in 1949 left them with 78 percent. But the elite Jordanian troops fought off the Jews and kept control of the Old City of Jerusalem, including the Jewish Section and the Wailing Wall.

Jews and Arabs fought, and each was able to keep what it could hold in battle. Neither side was completely happy with the outcome. Fair enough. But then we come to the question of the Muslims living in Palestine. In 1949, when the dust cleared from the fighting, there were about 155,000 Palestinians left within Israel. Only 17 percent of the Palestinians who had been living within the borders of what was now Israel were still there. Did the Jews force the Palestinians out? Or did they leave because their leaders told them to? Did the Jews terrorize them to make them leave? Was there a clear Jewish plan to remove them? Or were the Muslims leaving only in the hope of later ridding Palestine of all Jews?

Jews in Tel Aviv celebrating the news that the United Nations favored the partition of Palestine on November 29, 1947.

This is the heart of the historical problem of Israel. I would really like to believe that the Israelis did nothing wrong. Or I would like to be sure that they were terribly at fault, so that their obligation to the Palestinians was clear. I would love to know exactly how to fit what happened then into what I know of America's history of wars with the Indians, and enslavement of blacks. I wish I knew just how to compare the story of the Jewish state of Israel with the period of white rule in South Africa. I wish there was just one straightforward story of 1948 with a shining moral at the end. But there isn't.

We have gone from How did Israel come to be? to Why did the Palestinians lose their land? Finally we need to turn our eyes to April 9, 1948, in a village that no longer exists. I know the area well, for I have driven by it often, passing the thick-walled homes built by the Arabs and the old Christian monasteries, steering around the large buses of tourists from throughout the world. These are the Jerusalem hills, which sunset bathes in a golden light. I look forward to staying with my nearby relatives in Ein Kerem, sharing the warmth and company of three generations sprawled over two connected homes. But I am also driving past the site of a massacre.

On April 9, Jews murdered Arabs in the village of Deir Yassin. The elders of Deir Yassin had refused to aid the forces fighting against the Jews. In fact, they had a pact with a nearby Jewish village to keep the peace. But other Arabs had attacked Jews near Jerusalem, and the most militant Jews—the same faction that had bombed the King David Hotel—decided to take over the village. The leader of that terrorist splinter group was Menachem Begin, who later became prime minister of Israel and won the Nobel Peace Prize for signing a peace treaty with Egypt.

Perhaps 120 villagers were killed that day, including the elderly, women, and children. There was a battle for the village, and some claim there were soldiers from other Arab nations in the area. But even if a few of the deaths resulted from combat, most historians agree that Jews deliberately massacred Arabs in Deir Yassin, and then paraded some of the captured and defeated Arabs through Jewish neighborhoods in Jerusalem.

Does the massacre at Deir Yassin mean that, more generally, Jews terrorized the Palestinians into running away? The Israeli historian Benny Morris found that Deir Yassin was not unique. He uncovered twenty-four cases during the war in which Jews assaulted or murdered Palestinians, driving them out of their homes; he even tracked down a few cases of Jews raping Palestinian women. These attacks sent the message to Muslims that they were in great danger unless they fled from their homes.

There are those who claim the Jews were following a detailed strategy (called Plan Dalet, or Plan D) to destroy Arab villages and force out the Palestinians. Today we call that "ethnic cleansing"— driving entire peoples out of their homes so that the remaining group can have the whole nation to themselves. Most historians do not believe the Jews were that cold-blooded, or that the Jews alone were responsible for the flight of the Muslims. (Israeli Jewish scholars have been among the most outspoken in arguing that driving out the Palestinians was a calculated effort at "ethnic cleansing," and gentile outsiders, with no direct stake in this debate, have been more skeptical.)

I am sure that the Palestinians abandoning their homes and fields pleased many Jews. I am also sure that in attacking Palestinians quite a few Jewish soldiers must have wanted to spread fear. But Palestinians had also massacred and hoped to terrorize Jews, both before and during the war. Indeed, Haji Amin al-Husayni, the most important leader of the Muslims in Palestine, rushed to Germany during World War II. There, he did everything he could to help the Nazis and to rally Arabs to their cause. He was the voice of all the Arabs who had never accepted British rule, and wanted to turn the clock back to conditions as they had existed before World War I. He also did his best to make sure no Palestinians remained as neighbors to Jews. Other Muslim leaders told, retold, and exaggerated the story of Deir Yassin, reporting 254 deaths, and making up gruesome stories of mutilations by Jewish soldiers. If Jews wanted to terrorize Muslims into leaving, Muslim leaders also wanted to stampede Muslims so that they would not remain and make their peace with the Jews.

We know about the Jewish crimes because the Israeli government files were opened and Israeli historians have been diligent in reading them and honest about what they found. There has not been any similar investigation by Palestinian historians. We simply do not know in detail about the mood, the hopes, and the fears of the Palestinians. So we cannot say with certainty how many of the Palestinians were set on eliminating their Jewish neighbors, or how many would have been willing to stay and live with the Jews, if they had not been pushed to leave by their fellow Palestinians.

Palestinians call the fighting in this period and the loss of so many homes and fields "al-Nakba," the catastrophe. In some ways it might have been called "the inevitable." Jews were determined to have their own state. They were headed toward that one goal, fueled by nationalism, by the pioneer spirit, by two thousand years of yearning, and by the recent raw memory of the Holocaust. With that attitude, many—most—of the Jews must have wished the Arabs would disappear.

There were a few outspoken Israelis, such as the philosopher

Martin Buber, who were against any form of separation. Buber insisted that the new state must be shared between Jews and Palestinians. To this day there are Israelis who look back to Buber's humane voice and feel the country should have listened to him. Most Jews, though, expected some form of partition. Jews wanted as much good land as they could get. But they expected a version of the India–Pakistan partition to take place in Palestine. Yet, to this day, the Palestinians do not have a functioning state. Why is that?

As far as I can tell, no one in the Arab or Palestinian leadership accepted the idea of partition. The founder of Pakistan, Muhammad Ali Jinnah, seeing that the English were going to leave India, was skilled, relentless, and practical in carving out a Muslim state. True, Muslims were a minority in India and a majority in Palestine. But to my knowledge there was no Jinnah in the Arab or Palestinian leadership. Had there been a leader with a hard practical view of how to make the best of the changing circumstances, the Palestinians would have come away with a state of their own decades ago.

Jews did terrorize Palestinians during the war, and that did reflect a basic attitude of wishing that Israel could just be a Jewish state. But Palestinians who had not accepted the changed circumstances in the region since the end of the Ottoman Empire were equally trapped by their beliefs. They did not negotiate for a better deal, and they refused any agreement that granted the Jews a state.

Anwar Nusseibeh—who had lost a leg in a battle for Jerusalem, who knew Haji Amin al-Husayni personally, whose family still held the key to the Church of the Holy Sepulcher—sadly recognized these failings. He wrote in his diary: "My fault lay in my overweening conceit and in this I speak of myself as the average man. I underestimated the strength of my enemy and overestimated the strength of my own people . . . I thought too much in terms of the past glories of my people and willfully blinded myself to present shortcomings." With this kind of thinking the most surprising thing is not that the overwhelming majority of Palestinians fled, or were driven out, but that so many stayed within Israel. The Palestinians who remained are the parents and grandparents of the Arab citizens of Israel I mentioned at the beginning of this book.

Still, after all these explanations, I find Deir Yassin disturbing. Nothing can take away the discomfort of knowing that Israel was born at the price of so many people losing their homes. The site of the village is now a mental hospital, which I pass by while driving to visit my relatives in Ein Kerem.

Technically Ein Kerem is part of Jerusalem, but it looks and feels like a small Arab village, which it was before 1948. The domed houses the Arabs built are like large stones set into the hills. You feel that the people who built them were so much a part of that soil that they grew their homes, the way a snail grows a shell. The walls are so thick that they act as a form of air-conditioning, keeping the inner rooms cool. The houses, as one relative of mine pointed out, all face inward: Life is inside, where the family lives.

By law, all new buildings in Jerusalem must be made out of the sandy colored stone of the Jerusalem hills. The yellow-golden color, the crags and crevices in the stone, tie the whole city together, as if the buildings were quarried out of the hills. Yet looming over the city is the ugliest new high-rise apartment: the Holy Land Complex. The building is an eyesore, as if an overly proud parent had jabbed a mammoth 2 candle on a toddler's tiny pink birthday cupcake. Or, more accurately, as if a developer had flown over Miami Beach, picked up a gigantic new hotel, and dropped it down in ancient Jerusalem.

The building is all wealth displayed to the outside world, the opposite of the Arab buildings.

The Arabs nestled in where nature allowed, their eyes on their families and clans, while the Jews passed laws, built a modern nation, and imposed their will on the land. That makes it all the more painful to think that the Arabs are gone—these people who were so much of that one particular place—the one place in the world they cannot go.

And yet, one side of my family that lives in Ein Kerem is headed by a landscape architect who has devoted his life to respecting the land and history of Israel, but in modern ways, using modern means. The other side includes another landscape architect who is extremely active in politics, defending the rights of Palestinians.

The storm that pulled the Palestinians out of their homes was not just Jewish will; it was modern times. If there were no Jews at all in what is now Israel, you can be sure some Saudi developer would be building the same ugly buildings. And, as actually happened during the mandate, rich Muslim landowners would be selling off beautiful old homes to the highest bidders.

Israel is haunted by the dead of the Holocaust, and by the homes and memory of the Palestinians who once lived there. Dina Peleg was born in France, managed to evade the Nazis, then moved to Israel after the war. She puts it very well: "I think you have two types of Holocaust survivor: those who say it must not happen again and those who are afraid to lose their human face." That is the challenge of Israel: to be strong and protect Jews, and to save its human face, its essential humanity.

Israel is the product of hard calculations, and idealistic dreams; it offers a shelter, a refuge, to Jews who have been the victims of discrimination, and it discriminates against its Arab citizens; it bristles with weapons to make sure Jews will never again face death camps, and it struggles to save its humanity, its conscience, its heart. Of course that mixture of pragmatism and idealism is equally true of the United States.

ONE MORE AMERICAN PARALLEL

When you criticize Israeli Jews for depriving the many Arabs of their homes in 1948, someone will quickly bring up the destruction of the Indians in America. Who are you to judge? they are saying. You got North America because you killed the Indians. I think the parallel is not as close as it seems, but it suggests another that is more useful.

Historians estimate that the native population of the Americas declined by about 90 percent after the Europeans arrived. "Declined" is such a faceless word—no one is responsible, there are no dead babies, no tortured fathers, no sobbing mothers. It leaves out the contempt of Europeans who thought of the peoples of America as subhuman, worked them to death, cheated, murdered, and lied to grab native lands—and then viewed people robbed of their homes as a doomed race, fit only to dwindle away on barren reservations. Yet I chose this word deliberately. By far the largest reason for the Native American tragedy was disease. Certainly the destruction of the Indians was convenient for the European settlers, who enslaved, abused, and massacred them. But neither people understood how diseases such as smallpox were transmitted. By the late 1700s the English knew more, and some English soldiers did give blankets infected with smallpox to the Indians to spread disease. But the major damage to the Indian population had already been done by then.

If the native peoples of the Americas had been resistant to the new diseases, the Europeans might have been even more ruthless. But that is speculation. After all, in Africa and India, where the Europeans were brutal rulers but the native population was not as susceptible to disease, the Europeans eventually had to give up and leave. They may have wanted to wipe out the people they met, but they chose to rule, not to exterminate. If it is fair to term the deaths of the natives of the Americas a genocide, it is a genocide primarily caused by viruses and germs.

Because so many Indians died out or fled, the Europeans could not use them as slaves. Instead, they imported people from Africa, which suggests a different parallel between American history and that of Israel. Thomas Jefferson spoke of slavery as having "the wolf by the ear." That is, slaves could neither be kept in bondage nor freed. So he, and others like him, suggested returning blacks to Africa. But the plan never worked. Black Americans did not want to go, just as the Arab citizens of Israel want to remain in their home country. The great composer and band leader Duke Ellington put it perfectly. Speaking for all black Americans, he said, "We are something apart, yet an integral part." I think the lesson of American history for Israelis is that, however much racism and tension there is in America, blacks and whites prefer to live in the nation they built together.

REFUGEE

Some seven hundred thousand residents of Palestine fled during the war that established modern Israel. Leaving behind homes where generations of people had lived, the Palestinians rushed east across the Jordan River to towns along its west bank, or farther into Jordan, away from the Israeli army, or south into Gaza, or north into Lebanon and Syria. Those refugees are the parents and grandparents of the more than four million Palestinian refugees who still live in camps to this day. Their fate is one last question to consider in this first section. Why should a problem that was created sixty years ago still be with us today? Who is at fault?

For a long time, the attitude of the Jews was: You chose to leave, you hoped to destroy us, we can never let you back. And the Jews used the Palestinians' own argument against them: If Palestine really was part of Greater Syria, or of a united Muslim realm stretching from Egypt to Iraq, the people who fled should be comfortable anywhere in that territory. This attitude ignored the attachment people have to their particular homes, where generations of their relations lived their lives. Israel was founded on the yearning of the Jewish people to return home after two thousand years, yet the Jews were remarkably deaf to the same yearning on the part of the Palestinians, who held— and still hold—the keys to their old houses.

And yet blaming the misery of the refugees on heartless Jews is simplistic. Through very great effort, the Jews created a nation. They built farms to feed themselves, cities to foster business and govern- ment, armies to defend themselves. They revived biblical Hebrew, which was like Latin, a language known only by scholars, and made it into a modern language that they taught to all Israelis. After the birth of Israel, attacks against Jews living in Muslim countries became more and more frequent. The Israelis accepted some half a million Jewish refugees from Muslim lands into Israel. From the Israeli point of view, they coped with their own refugee problem.

From Herzl on, the modern Zionists were Europeans. Jews whose families lived in Europe are called "Ashkenazi Jews." The word itself traces back to an older form of the word for "Germany" in Hebrew. Until they came to Israel, most Ashkenazi Jews spoke Yiddish, which is so close to German that my mother, who speaks German but not Yiddish, can understand it. The overwhelming majority of Jews who came to America were from this background, and so it is easy to think of Ashkenazi Jews as all Jews. But there were lots of other Jews in the world who were neither Ashkenazi nor Yiddish speakers.

A large group of Jews had lived in Spain until they were expelled in 1492. They spoke Ladino, a language similar to Spanish, and they are known as Sephardic Jews. And then there were the Jews from throughout the lands of the Middle East, Central Asia, and even India. Today the term for that group of Jews is "Mizrahi"—"Eastern"—Jews. When the Jewish refugees flooded in to Israel after 1948, many were Mizrahi Jews.

Azhkenazi Jews included Germans who understood the work of Albert Einstein and were creating the very latest advances in physics, mathematics, and chemistry. By contrast, when airplanes arrived in Yemen, the local Jews did not know what they were. Many of the European Jews were completely at home in the art and culture of western Europe, and were as familiar with Plato, Shakespeare, and Tolstoy as they were with the Bible. Many of the Mizrahi Jews could not read. Although both groups were officially Jews, they could not have been more different. The Ashkenazi Jews were certain that the differences were a sign of their superiority.

Here's another family story, which gives a picture of how prejudiced Ashkenazi Jews were against Mizrahi Jews. Avram, my grandfather Solomon's eldest son, married a gentile. Nina converted, but the angry rabbi would not accept his son and daughter-in-law until he lay dying. Avram's own daughter, Naomi, later eloped with a Yemeni Jew. From the standpoint of most Ashkenazis, her rebellion was as extreme as her father's. I recently heard a similar story from an Israeli friend. In the 1950s an Ashkenazi daughter was beaten by her father for dating a Mizrahi. But the forbidden lovers eventually married, and my friend is their grandson. In a sense that family history is the broader story of the two kinds of Jews in Israel: there were, and still are, clashes between the Europeans and the Middle Easterners, but ultimately the nation accepted the refugees and added them into the mix of the Israeli population.

The Muslim nations on Israel's borders did not have the same view of Palestinians. Palestinian refugees were not allowed to settle in the half of Jerusalem that their own brother Palestinians controlled. To this day, only Jordan allows Palestinian refugees to become full citizens. The Arab nations permitted refugee camps to be built, but were dead set against either letting the refugees leave their camps to find their way to better lives, or encouraging the refugees to take a pragmatic, practical approach to building a Palestinian state. They wanted the Palestinians to be angry, furious at Israel, and insistent on returning home.

As we have seen, the Israelis are tough, determined, practical, if at times also callous. The Palestinians have been impractical, focused on completely reversing existing conditions, and thus given to anger. In a way, the Israelis keep saying, This is what is, what are you going to do about it? The Palestinians keep saying, You could have done it differently, so why should we cooperate?

These two attitudes come together in one phrase often used by the Palestinians: "the right of return." A brilliant choice of words, for it directly echoes a phrase first used by the Israelis, who offer "the right of return" to a Jew anywhere in the world. He or she can automatically become a citizen of Israel. Well, the Palestinians say, if Jews can "return" after two thousand years, why can't we after sixty?

The Israeli response is typically practical: If four million Palestinians returned to Israel, joining the one million Arabs and five million Jews already there, the Jewish state would disappear. I think the Israelis are right on this issue. While in the 1950s and early '60s, America urged Israel to accept the refugees, that is no longer realistic. There is not a single nation on this Earth that would willingly open its borders to such a huge and angry refugee population. In fact, throughout the world, nations are now tightening their laws, restricting immigration. And Arab nations that have forbidden Palestinians refugees, even those born on their own soil, to become citizens have no right to criticize Israel. Why should Israel be asked to do what no other nation would? But the suffering of the Palestinian refugees is real, and the Israelis did play a crucial part in causing their pain and displacement.

In some negotiations, the Israelis have suggested paying compensation to Palestinians who lost homes and land. In a 2003 poll taken by a respected Palestinian pollster, an astonishing 70 percent of the refugees surveyed said if they had the opportunity they would accept money and the chance to live in a Palestinian state, and would give up the right of return. Only 10 percent felt that they needed to return to their homes in what is now Israel.

In reality, the issue of return may well be solvable. But reality only goes so far in this conflict. On the one hand, Palestinians were furious at the pollster when the results were announced. They acted as if he had betrayed his own people by revealing their flexibility. On the other hand, I have often heard Israelis justify harsh measures against

Palestinians by saying, Look, they insist on their right of return, they want to destroy us. The Israelis are just as ready to ignore the poll results. Both sides would rather hold on to their fears and furies than reach an agreement. And compensation alone is only part of the issue.

Abu Ramsi is a Palestinian whom we might call a village elder, known for his skill at settling disputes. He told the American reporter Richard Ben Cramer that "What the Jews do not understand is, first, they have to *apologize*—for taking the land, for dispossessing the Arabs, and brutalizing the Palestinian people. Because without the restoration of honor, then you cannot move on to the division according to rights." Sari Nusseibeh agrees. As he explained to a Jewish audience in Israel, "It doesn't matter whether you set out premeditatedly to cause the Palestinian refugee tragedy . . . The tragedy did occur, even as an indirect consequence of your actions. In our tradition you have to own up to this. You have to come and offer an apology." On this, I think the Palestinians are right.

REFUGEE

II. Israel Is Born—What Is Israel?

THE DAYS OF DAVID

We have come from Herzl to the Holocaust, from Israel as a dream to its beginnings as a state. All along, Zionists were sure that Jews needed a nation, while American Jews believed they needed to be accepted as citizens of the United States. Once Israel became a reality—a nation in the world, no longer just a dream or a yearning—Israeli Jews faced a new set of unsettling questions. On the one hand, the newly born country experienced the daily challenge of mere survival—from not only the threat of potential new wars, but the challenge of feeding, clothing, and housing its citizens. On the other hand, the socialist Zionists who ran Israel needed to decide how their nation could be Jewish but democratic; a homeland for Jews but also a state governed by modern laws that apply equally to all, no matter whether they are Jewish, Muslim, Christian, Buddhist, pagan, or totally antireligious.

When I picture the founding of Israel, I think of Miriam Groag's husband Willie; he was the most determined man I've ever met, and the most willing to sacrifice for his ideals. Willie had a full head of the kind of white hair that looks handsome on a man—somewhere

Willie and his second wife, Tamar, on Ma'anit, the kibbutz where I met them years later.

between rumpled and distinguished. He always had a half smile, a glint in his eye, a sense of humor about the world. You see that even in the drawings Willie made in the concentration camp at Terezin. Indeed, it was Willie who rescued the drawings made by the children of the camp, which were later published as *I Never Saw a Butterfly*.

I brought Marina, my wife, to meet Willie the year after we were married, when he was in his eighties, living with Tamar, his second wife, on the same kibbutz. They had a neat garden apartment in a long single-story building that looked like a small college dorm: a row of identical doors, functional, nothing fancy, but fine. He accepted the small home the way he accepted his assignment to this kibbutz. The good of the group is what mattered to him. I'd heard that Willie was having health problems, and you could tell he had a bum leg. A golf cart was parked outside the door, so he could speed around to see his kids and grandkids. But then he got up and said he needed to show us something.

The house was in a valley, facing a long slope. Willie marched ahead of us, faster than we could go, up the red soil hillside dotted with scrub brush. We kept wondering about that leg. But as he strode ahead, all you could see was his determination. When bushes blocked the way, he pushed them aside. Nothing could stop him. He paused only to pick up a handful of earth and show us the many shards of Roman pottery in it. He wanted us to see that we were standing on ancient history. And something more: down a ravine, then up a steeper hill. We reached the crest, he brushed aside a gnarled, knobby branch, and suddenly we could see way down a valley. "There," he said, "right there, was where we fought in 1948."

Willie was not bragging. In fact, Marina and I noticed something sad and wistful about his expression. He remembered when the Arabs were here, as neighbors—even if there were clashes—and not far off, across borders. Willie was not taking us there to say anything bad about Arabs. He just needed to show what he himself had built.

Willie made himself walk up that hill. Reaching the top, telling us that story, was much more important then resting his leg. That was the pioneer spirit of the kibbutz. He was not bitter about the Nazis. He missed living near the Arabs. He never complained about the kibbutz that told him where to live and work. He did not want revenge or triumph or money. He wanted to create a better home in the world. And he did.

Think of the challenges Israel faced just after it was born: needing to absorb those masses of refugees—first Holocaust survivors, then Mizrahi Jews expelled from Muslim countries; finding a consistent and protected supply of water; building roads and cities. Just born as a nation, Israel needed to provide for the education, health, and safety of its people, even as its hostile neighbors refused to recognize that it existed, and were arming themselves to the teeth. As Israelis tamed their land, nurtured their people, and prepared to defend themselves, they also had to work out the rules they would live by. There had not been a Jewish nation for two thousand years, so what rules should Israel follow?

To give you a sense of how the founders of Israel thought religion would fit into the state, I'll begin with my favorite aunt, Riva; my grandfather's youngest daughter. Riva was that rare sort of woman who pays no attention to how she looks. She wore no makeup. Her hair circled her head, thick strands of gray and black flying this way and that. The wrinkles and lines of her face were there to see; she made no effort to hide them. She smoked all the time. In other words, she resembled one of Israel's prime ministers: Golda Meir.

Riva and Golda actually had a lot in common, and were good

Prime Minister David Ben-Gurion with Mrs. Golda Meir at the Knesset, the Israeli Parliament, which is similar to our Congress.

friends. They were born in the same place, Kiev, within a few years of each other. They were teachers for a time, and they both worked in Israeli organizations to help women and children. They were smart, caring—in a tough-minded way. They were engineers, organizers, managers—not soft, soothing moms.

Observant Jews keep kosher, following strict rules on what they can and cannot eat, and how their food must be prepared. Riva once explained to me why the Jews came up with those laws: It was because uncooked pork could make you sick. Kosher was really a health plan. That was pure Riva, seeing religion as a way smart people in earlier times tried to improve their society, their community, just as she did every day. She was in Israel because she had been a good daughter. That is, instead of getting married and starting her own family, she took care of her aging parents until they died, then she was always the helpful aunt to other relatives while she worked in social service, providing for other families.

In my mind, Riva was the Israel of the 1950s and '60s: not glamorous, but smart, socially conscious, rational, soulful. Israel was to be something like Sweden or Denmark, or maybe the Upper West Side of Manhattan, where I lived, or the twin cities in Minnesota, or Madison, Wisconsin; a land where you paid high taxes, the government took care of you, and everyone was rational and progressive. Passover was a holiday celebrating Jews as fighters, the birth of Israel, and the rights of workers; it had little or nothing to do with God. Ultra-Orthodox believers were curiosities—local color you might point out when visiting old synagogues. They were part of the scenery that showed you were in the Holy Land.

The belief that Israel should be a land of reason in which Judaism is another form of progressive thinking is still held by many Israelis.

But you would not know it from the rules of Israeli society. For example, marriage in Israel is left entirely in the hands of the most devout rabbis. Most everything shuts down on Saturday, the Jewish Sabbath. Even though most Israelis do not bother with keeping kosher at home, the army serves kosher food. These laws were passed because of the way politics is structured in Israel.

In America only two parties ever have a chance to win national elections. Once the votes are counted, we know who is president and which party has a majority in the House or Senate. In Israel, there are many more parties. And it is not clear who will actually be in power until those parties make deals with one another and form coalitions. From the very beginning of Israel, parties with strong religious views have been key coalition partners. So while most Israelis shared my aunt Riva's views, the Israeli government adopted more and more religious laws.

The clearest way to see how the antireligious rationality of the Zionists was undermined is through the story of Israel's army.

David Ben-Gurion was the George Washington of Israel. He served as Israel's prime minister from its founding in 1948 until 1963, with only a short break from 1953 to 1955. Ben-Gurion loved the army, and he explained why: "I see in the military not only the fortress that secures us . . . but an educational force for raising up the Jewish man, a cement for bringing together the nation, and a faithful mechanism for the absorption of immigrants." To this day, the army is viewed exactly this way, as the melting pot that takes individuals and forges them into citizens of Israel. Indeed, although Ben-Gurion said "the Jewish man," Jewish women serve in the army alongside their brothers. The experience of having served in the army really is meant to bind all Israeli Jews together. Ben-Gurion, though, decided that some Jews would not have to serve in the army at all.

Prime Minister Ben-Gurion and his wife visiting a kibbutz in 1954. In the new state of Israel, even the head of the country was eager to show that he was still a farmer at heart.

In the early days of Israel, religious leaders appealed to Ben-Gurion to exempt the few students who were devoting their lives to religious texts from military service. Religious Jews who had rejected Zionism and kept waiting for the call of the Messiah were slaughtered by Hitler. As a result, there were only a handful of draft-age Jewish religious students. In 1954, Ben-Gurion agreed to exempt them from military service. His decision made sense at the time, but it was also a hint of the problem of having a state linked with a religion. Since then, demands by the religious to impose special rules have only grown louder.

ISRAEL AND HER ENEMIES: DAVID AND GOLIATH

The rabbis who asked to exempt their students from military service claimed that their prayers were the country's best defense. Luckily for Israel, Ben-Gurion put his trust in training and guns, not prayers. From 1948 on, the tiny state faced armed, determined enemies. In the Bible story, little David defeats the giant Goliath because he is smart enough—and brave enough—to use a slingshot; cleverness and will bring down the muscle-bound brute. Ben-Gurion and his Israel seemed to perfectly match that fable, as the tiny nation used its brains and determination to hold off the angry giants that threatened from all sides. Ben-Gurion himself was short, tough, and determined— a perfect David.

Little David—the Israel of Ben-Gurion—was both weak and strong. When the charismatic Moshe Dyan—equally famous for his eye patch, his popularity with women, and his record as head of the Israeli Army—visited Washington in 1953, he warned that Israel was extremely vulnerable. He also insisted that it could destroy all of the

Arab armies. Somehow Israel was both in danger and in command, which meant that it needed and deserved outside support. But who could young Israel count on as an ally?

Today, a reader seeing this question might think: America, of course—but that was not self-evident when Israel was born. American troops liberated concentration camps after World War II, and Americans back home saw photos of the victims. But that did not change American immigration laws. The quotas designed to keep out Jews stayed the same. And when President Truman suggested that the British take a hundred thousand of the miserable Jewish concentration camp victims and refugees into Palestine (before Israel was born), the British set up one commission after another to study the problem, and did nothing. America neither cared enough to welcome the starving victims of the Holocaust, nor to twist England's arm to let them into Palestine. So how much could America be trusted to risk for Israel? And anyone could see that oil was coming to mean more and more to car-mad America. A nation that needed oil might be inclined to favor oil-rich Arab states.

Israelis could not even entirely count on American Jews. Zionists were determined and proud, for they were creating a nation out of pure willpower. And they were not shy about saying that Jews belonged in Israel. Ben-Gurion appealed to American Jewish parents to "help us bring their children here." But he was not just asking politely, he was also warning that Israelis would do their best to turn young American Jews into Zionist Israelis. "Even if they decline to help, we will bring the youth to Israel." American Jews felt equally proud of having made their mark on the United States. They did not like the idea of a Zionist pied piper taking away their kids, or being told they were less Jewish for being American. In 1950 the president of the American

Jewish Committee insisted that "to American Jews, America is home." That was a direct rejection of the Zionist argument that a Jew could only be at home in his homeland.

American Jews were the ones who had said no to Zionism. Israeli Jews were the ones who had chosen not to move to America (or had been excluded from it). In the early days of the state of Israel, it was not clear how this gap, this history, could be overcome. Where could Israelis look for support outside of America?

The Soviet Union called itself a communist nation, which was close enough to the socialism favored by many Israeli pioneers. Indeed, the Soviet Union was the second country to recognize Israel after America. But by the 1950s the Soviets were seeing more to be gained in courting the many angry Arabs who controlled large armies and oil wells than the few Jews with their small country.

The Soviet Union was out, England (which had been only too happy to leave Palestine) was not even worth considering, and America was all good intentions with no results. Where could young Israel buy ammunition and find protection? In the 1950s the answer was clear: France. The French were still competing with the English for influence in the Middle East. They decided to be Israel's ally and arms supplier, an alliance that helped drag Israel into its first major war.

When Gamal Abdel Nasser became the leader of Egypt in 1954, he shook up the Middle East. Nasser tried to unite the Arab peoples against Israel, against the West, as a political bloc of their own. Then he announced that the Suez Canal, the crucial waterway that carried so much European shipping, belonged to Egypt.

England and France hated what Nasser was doing, so they hit upon a scheme. First, Israel would attack Egypt and take the canal. That would be good for Israel, which could sweep away the guerillas who were using the Sinai Peninsula as a base, and ensure that Israeli ships could use the Red Sea. Then France and England would rush in as if to restore order—but, really, so that they could regain control of the canal, while making Nasser look weak.

On the last days of October 1956, Israeli forces dashed across the Sinai and neared the canal. By November 5, the supposedly peace-making French and British soldiers began to arrive. But no one was fooled. America was especially furious. Here were the old colonial powers using the worst kinds of tricks for their own selfish interests. Pressure from America forced England and France to leave, and the canal remained in Egypt's hands. But America agreed to back Israel if the Egyptians again blocked Israeli ships. Scheming with France and England had failed, but Israel found its best ally. From the Suez crisis on, Israel and America drew ever closer. So did American and Israeli Jews.

HOME AND HOMELAND: THE NEW ANSWER FOR JEWS

Even as Israel faced dire military threats, Israelis struggled to build a nation and absorb hundreds of thousands of poor, battered Jews. These struggles gave American Jews a new way to think about the Zionist nation. You had to root for a country that was trying so hard, doing so much, beating the odds.

Willie and the many other men and women like him in that found-ing generation made Israel very easy to like. When the hundreds of thousands of newcomers who rushed to Israel after 1948 arrived in the new land, they were sent to an *ulpan*, a school for learning Hebrew. In my New York Sunday school we studied Hebrew with the same blue books used in the *ulpans*. As we memorized Hebrew words, we saw a smiling blue stick figure in the margins, pointing the way. That bright, appealing young man stood for Israel.

In the mid-1950s, Israel became a homeland for American Jews the way Italy is for Italian Americans, or Ireland for Irish Americans. The original homelands of those American Jews—Russia, Poland, Germany and the rest of Europe—no longer had many or even any Jews at all. There were Jewish cemeteries; there were memorials to Jewish communities that longer existed; there were concentration camps turned into museums. But that was a landscape of absence and death. If an American Jew wanted a link to a vibrant Jewish community outside America, he or she looked not to Europe but to Israel. So while Israel was a very new nation, it took the place of the mother country that other immigrant Americans honored. And as archaeologists dug in the Holy Land and found records of biblical cities, Israel seemed all the more the ancestral home for American Jews, even if their ancestors had left thousands of years before.

What a perfect combination: Israel gave American Jews "roots," and at the same time it was a lively, bright newcomer where Jews were building a nation. From young people in American Hebrew schools saving their dimes and nickels to Plant a Tree in Israel to large well-funded donation campaigns, American Jews sent their money to help build Israel. Israel needed the money, and was ready to stop arguing about where Jews belonged. American Jews were glad to feel they were contributing to Israel, could visit from time to time to see the ancient sites, and could return home to America feeling linked to the Jewish homeland. This was the happiest of long-distance marriages.

For me, growing up, Israel was the perfect David, the underdog you could feel proud about supporting. Here was a country the size of New Jersey, surrounded by hostile neighbors, that was doing nothing but good—building homes, providing for refugees, taking in Jewish orphans, draining swamps, growing its own food, even shipping its Jaffa oranges overseas; bringing science and medicine to a backward part of the world. And it faced a perfect Goliath. Nasser linked Egypt and Syria into one United Arab Republic. He hoped to keep adding more countries, until all the Arab peoples were joined together. Then they would descend in a fierce army to drive Israelis into the sea.

For me and many other American Jews, being for Israel and against the Arabs was like being for Martin Luther King Jr. and against segregation. In 1960 it was like being for the young, idealistic Democrat John F. Kennedy and against the dark and calculating Republican Richard M. Nixon. And when Kennedy was elected president he made the connection explicit. America, he said, "has a special relationship with Israel." If Israel were invaded, it was "quite clear" to him that America would come to its aid. Being for Israel was like being for every spunky young outsider hero who ever faced off against a mammoth and glowering enemy. One enemy was the Arabs. The other was the Nazi past.

THE MAN IN THE GLASS BOX

I have two cousins named Shlomo (the Hebrew equivalent of "Solomon," after our grandfather) and both were deeply affected by the Holocaust. The turning point for one came because of a trial he was covering as a journalist. The accused man, who sat in a glass box, exposed for all to see, was Adolf Eichman, architect of Hitler's Final Solution. Eichman had been hiding out in Argentina when, in May of 1960, the Israelis found him, captured him, and brought him back to face judgment.

The entire world watched the Eichman trial. This trim man with his neatly combed back hair was the face of ultimate evil. Yet Eichman did not resemble a TV maniac, or a movie villain like Hannibal Lecter or Voldemort. He was cold, precise, and distant. And he insisted that he was not a bad man, just a good German who followed orders and did as he was told. That is what made him truly terrifying, for he could have been anyone who put being efficient ahead of being human. The trial showed that evil exists in all of us. And it changed the meaning of the Holocaust in Israel.

Israel did not even have an official Holocaust Remembrance Day until 1959 (after America and France had already established remembrance days), but the Eichman trial opened the doors of memory throughout the country. As people came and testified against him, mothers, fathers, aunts, cousins, began to tell their stories. The nightmare memories of the Holocaust that people had been holding inside started to tumble out. Israelis stopped speaking of the Holocaust as a sign that European Jews had made the wrong choice. Instead they recognized it as the tragedy that linked the family histories of most of the Ashkenazi Jews. Shlomo the journalist turned historian went on to devote his life to researching and understanding the Holocaust. (In fact, it is his prize-winning work that I relied on when I said that FDR could only get America to enter World War II by not making it a war over the Jews.)

Today the Holocaust is taught in every American school. Holocaust museums, books, documentaries, and memorials can be found throughout the country. But it is different in Israel, where it is very likely that someone you are standing next to was directly touched by the Holocaust. This is a country where the Holocaust is personal. Indeed, the story of the Holocaust has become central to the meaning of Israel.

If you go to Yad Vashem, the Israeli Museum dedicated to the

This lovely image of a religious man and a young couple facing the picture window at Yad Vashem captures the message of the museum: out of the death and destruction of the Holocaust come the hope of life and faith in Israel. Critics point out that the village of Deir Yassin, where Jews massacred Arabs in 1948, would have been in the sightlines of that window, if it still existed. Israel is a state like any other, but, to their credit, Israeli Jews constantly question their own nation's moral foundations.

Holocaust, you will have two unforgettable experiences. In photos, captions, and objects, you see and hear how the Jews of Europe were murdered, as well as how some fought back and how others managed to survive. But the very ground you stand on tells another story.

My other cousin Shlomo, who designed the landscape architecture for the museum, explained that you are never to feel steady. You stand on a floor that is deliberately angled a tiny bit, so you feel slightly queasy as you move through the installations until, at the very end of the exhibit, you walk up a slant, a rise. Then, finally, you arrive on a level floor to face a large bay window, looking out on the land of Israel. The story the layout of the museum tells is that Jews can never be steady, never be safe, unless or until they live in Israel; Israel is the answer to the tragedy of the Holocaust. (Israelis critical of their own country point out that when you look through that pane of glass, you are staring directly toward the site of Deir Yassin.)

Until the Eichman trial, individual Israelis, and Israel the nation, thought it best to look ahead, to focus on the future. The Holocaust was the tragic past. This is similar to the ways in which slavery was treated by many black families in America until the 1970s. Although they all knew about it, and perhaps passed along family stories, it was part of a past most preferred to leave behind. But when Alex Haley's *Roots* was made into a popular TV miniseries, more and more African Americans eagerly looked back to investigate their pasts and tell those stories. Slavery, a subject that had been kept private, now became public. In Israel, the Eichman trial and the opening of the doors of memory only confirmed what the Arab threats and the glorious growth of Israel suggested: Israel stood against evil, and for all that was good in the world. And then in six days in 1967, plucky, underdog David became the triumphant Goliath.

III. Did Winning the 1967 War Ruin Israel?

"OUR GOAL IS CLEAR—TO WIPE ISRAEL OFF THE FACE OF THE MAP"

In spring 1967, the Middle East was preparing for war. Syria was sponsoring attacks on Israel, which kept considering a punishing retaliation. The marriage of Egypt and Syria had fallen apart, but that only encouraged Nasser to show his strength in ever more vicious verbal attacks on America and Israel. *The Voice of the Arabs*, an Egyptian radio program he controlled, announced, "the sole method we shall apply against Israel is total war, which will result in the extermination of Zionist existence." The Israelis met threats with defiance. On May 15, Israel held an Independence Day parade in its half of Jerusalem. The parade was an announcement: "We are here and strong."

The whole region was on edge, like Southern California after many dry summers when even the air feels ready to burst into flames. Just then the Soviets dropped a match: They told the Egyptians a lie, claiming to have proof that the Israelis had massed fifteen brigades on the border of Syria, and were about to invade.

The Soviet report was a complete fabrication. Why would the

Soviets pass on false information, especially at a moment when it could do so much damage? To this day, no one knows. But perhaps it is like any situation in which rumors are flying, like a terrible game of Telephone. A lie that one person tells for his own reasons, spreads, grows, and soon becomes something else: an unstoppable momentum toward war. The Soviet lie made it seem that Israel was about to start a war, making it impossible for any Arab leader to show the slightest acceptance of Israel. Actually, it allowed every Arab state to act on its fondest wish.

Egypt, Syria, Jordan, Iraq, and the refugee Palestinians all wanted to destroy Israel. Both Egypt and Jordan had made secret contacts with the Israelis from time to time as various plans were floated to turn the truce that ended the 1948 war into a real peace settlement. But none of those discussions went anywhere. The simple truth is that the leaders of Israel's Arab neighbors, as well as most of the citizens of those nations, did not accept any of the pro-Jewish decisions made by the British or the United Nations, or the outcome of either the 1948 war or the Suez crisis in 1956. To them, Israel was a humiliation that must be utterly destroyed so completely that it would be as if the Jewish state had never existed.

The Egyptians moved men and planes closer to Israel, in attack position. The Jordanians put their forces under the control of an Egyptian general. The Iraqis sent more men and planes. The Syrians massed to follow their strategy for slicing Israel in half. In the last days of May, war was about to begin.

The president of Iraq announced, "our goal is clear—to wipe Israel off the face of the map." Ahmad al-Shuqayri, head of the Palestine Liberation Organization (for more on the PLO, see pages 114–16), warned that "we shall destroy Israel and its inhabitants and as for

the survivors—if there are any—the boats are ready to deport them."
When fighting started in Jerusalem, a loudspeaker on the Dome of the
Rock, the holy Muslim site, told the faithful, "we have waited years for
this battle to erase the stain of the past."

The Israelis knew exactly what was at stake. As one lieutenant
said, we were "thinking in terms of annihilation." Israel's prime minister agreed: "We are engaged in a life-or-death struggle to defend
our existence." The Israelis also knew that no country, not one single
nation, would help them. Israel had purchased most of its airplanes
from France. As war was about to break out, the French decided that
Arab oil meant more to them than Israeli money, and announced that
they would not supply the replacement parts the Israelis were sure
to need.

What about America? America had promised to protect Israeli
ships. But now the Americans said they would lend only moral
support unless the Israelis let the Muslims attack first. Surrounded,
facing enemies with double the number of planes, Israel saw its only
chance in the element of surprise, in dictating where and how the war
would start. The Americans understood, but said they could not help,
for they could not afford to ally themselves with the aggressor, even
though the Arabs were moving their troops and planes into position
to destroy Israel. For Jews both in and outside of Israel, this moment
was like the Holocaust all over again. The world could see the danger
to Israel, but Jews needed to fend for themselves.

On the morning of June 5, the war everyone knew was coming
began in a way no one expected. Israeli airplanes took to the skies in
two opposite directions: One wing went west over the Mediterranean
Sea, then swung sharply south into Egypt; another set off south before
splitting again, sending one arm directly into Egypt and another over

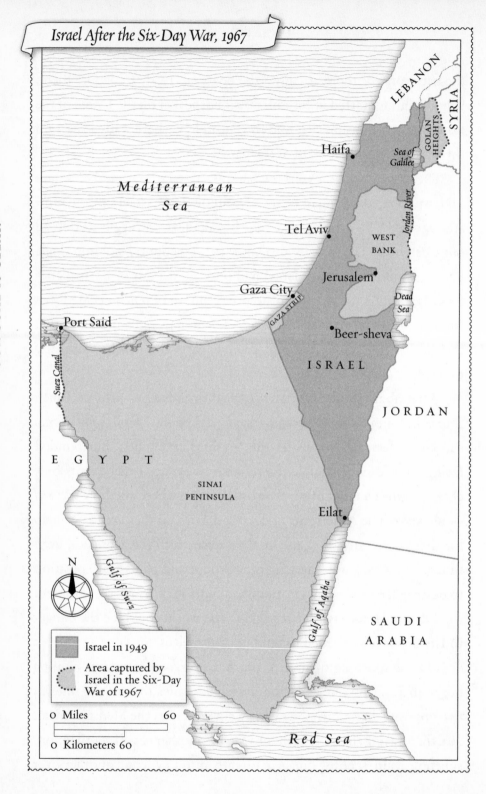

"OUR GOAL IS CLEAR"

LEBANON

SYRIA

GOLAN HEIGHTS

Haifa

Sea of Galilee

Mediterranean Sea

Jordan River

Tel Aviv

WEST BANK

Jerusalem

Gaza City

GAZA STRIP

Dead Sea

Port Said

Beer-sheva

ISRAEL

Suez Canal

JORDAN

E G Y P T

SINAI PENINSULA

Eilat

N

Gulf of Suez

Gulf of Aqaba

SAUDI ARABIA

Israel in 1949

Area captured by Israel in the Six-Day War of 1967

0   Miles   60

0   Kilometers 60

Red Sea

Jordan and Saudi Arabia, before diving down to another key Egyptian base. The planes flew so low that they were not picked up by radar, and arrived undetected and unopposed at every major Egyptian air base. In a little more than an hour, the Israelis destroyed half the Egyptian air force.

Smart, brave, well-trained, and lucky, the Israelis demolished their enemy's best weapons before they had even begun to fight.

You can see why Israel sees itself as both very weak and very strong. The whole world left Israel to fight off the armies of four nations and the PLO, all bent on obliterating the Jewish state. And in just over an hour of combat, Israel crippled the fighting capacity of its largest enemy. But the destruction of the Egyptian air force was just the beginning of the Israeli triumph. It was also the beginning of the Israeli tragedy.

OCCUPATION

During the 1967 War (known as the Six-Day War, because that is all the time it took for Israel to win) Israel not only defeated its enemies, but changed its borders. Israel took back East Jerusalem, the half of the city Jordan had managed to hold in 1948. Israeli troops arrived to discover that in the nineteen years of Jordanian rule the Jewish Quarter had been destroyed, and Jewish graves desecrated. But the Wailing Wall still stood and was now in Jewish hands. The Israelis took the Sinai Peninsula, the tiny Gaza Strip, and captured much of the West Bank of the Jordan, which included many towns mentioned in the Bible and linked to the most important Jewish historical figures. That also meant that the Israelis were now in charge of the one million

Palestinian refugees living on those newly captured lands. After a bloody fight, Israel soon also took the Golan Heights from Syria. In less than one week, Israel went from being a state threatened with annihilation to an occupier, ruling over many of the displaced Palestinians.

One way to picture the change that came with the Six-Day War is to think of the war America fought against Mexico in 1846. By taking control of California, Texas, and much of the Southwest, America clearly established that it would rule "from sea to shining sea." Many white Americans believed that the war proved the United States had a special destiny to rule all of North America, and perhaps more. Indeed, the war left seventy-five thousand Mexicans within a new country where they were often viewed as inferior.

Yet for all of that sense of triumph, the Mexican War broke America apart. Abraham Lincoln, for one, called the war immoral. That view was echoed by many abolitionists. As the Mexican lands were divided up into new states, the question immediately arose whether they would be slave or free, a dispute that led directly to the Civil War. And the Mexican War itself inspired Henry David Thoreau to write "On Civil Disobedience," an essay that insists an individual's conscience is more important than his responsibility to obey the law. Thoreau's essay eventually inspired Mohandas K. Gandhi to lead his nonviolent movement for the independence of India, which, in turn, gave a new direction to Martin Luther King Jr. and the Civil Rights movement in America. In one way, the Mexican War was the most vivid declaration of white Americans' belief in their natural superiority. In other way, the American takeover of Mexican lands inspired revulsion against that very prejudice.

Israel's victories in the Six-Day War had the same effects in Israel. Israelis began to speak of their destiny to rule all of the lands of their

Chief of Staff Yitzhak Rabin on the right, Minister of Defense Moshe Dyane in the center, and General Uzi Narkis on the left, entering the old city of Jerusalem. Before Israel won the Six-Day War, Jews could not enter East Jerusalem, so this was a triumphant moment for Israel. But figuring out what to do with the territory Israel conquered has deeply divided Israeli Jews.

fathers. But other Israelis cannot stand what occupation has done to their county, believing it has hardened the nation, turning its "human face" into a steel mask. "We are not meant to be occupiers," Dov's widow, Hannah, said to me one day, shaking her head. She sees Jewish morality fading, the Jewish heart toughening.

I feel presumptuous commenting on this, for I did not fight for Israel. But when the generation of Israelis who helped create the nation feels that the country is being ruined, I must listen. And that returns me to my big questions. It is one thing to admire how underdog Israel fought off its enemies and made itself strong. But what of conqueror Israel? Has Israel changed? Is that the fault of Palestinian rage and suicide bombs? Or has a brutal side of Israel that was not visible in its early days now emerged full-blown? If one set of questions about Israel relates to 1948—how the nation came to be and how the Palestinians lost their land—another set concerns what Israel has become since it won the 1967 war.

WHY SHOULD ISRAEL BE DIFFERENT FROM ANY OTHER CONQUEROR?

Most of the time I think occupation has poisoned Israel, as Frodo is corrupted by holding the Ring of Power in *The Lord of the Rings*. But I am not sure. Why should a state that defeated its most aggressive neighbors be forced to give back land won in battle? America had far less justification for fighting Mexico in 1846 than Israel did in defeating the Arabs in 1967. Yet no one believes America should, or would, give any land back to Mexico. Why should Israel be held to a different standard?

In 1967 the Arabs spoke in glowing terms about their plans to meet up in Tel Aviv or Haifa after driving the Jews into the sea. As Nasser's radio station made perfectly clear, their goal was the "extermination" of Jews in Israel. Had the Arabs won, they would never have shown any mercy to Jews, nor given an inch of land back. Why should the victorious nation be obliged to be generous, especially when the defeated enemy's entire goal was to destroy that country? That makes no sense. Holier-than-thou criticism of Israel both excuses the determination of the Arabs to wipe out Israel and ignores the actual history of every other nation. In fact, it is a form of anti-Semitism, because it demands more of Jews than of any-one else while ignoring or excusing the worst intentions of their enemies.

And yet I, like most Israelis, think the occupation is wrong and must end. Not just to bring peace, but for the sake of the Israelis themselves. Amram Mitza, a former general in the Israeli army, puts it this way: "the occupation is corrupting us. . . . We are behaving like the cruelest enemies the Jewish people ever had. You know people accuse us of behaving like Germans and we say 'no, we have morals, we don't put them in ghettoes.' The reality is that we are occupying three and a half million people against their will."

How could Israeli Jews wind up being accused of "behaving like Germans"? That is the poison of occupation: To rule over others you have conquered, you must either be so ruthless that you destroy their every hope of liberation, or so generous that you train them to replace you. But that choice is not clear right away. At first there is just the joy of victory.

THE JERUSALEM WONDERLAND?

In May of 1967, as war loomed, Jews from throughout the world rushed to Israel to fight, to help, to be part of the struggle. I was too young and scared to go. I took my second trip to Israel the following year, in 1968. By then the hard days of war were over, and I felt as if I had entered a wonderland.

To me, Jerusalem united and controlled by Israel was a kind of Disneyland: a place where dreams came true. Passing through the gates of the walled Old City was like entering the castle in the Magic Kingdom. Even getting lost in the maze of cobblestone streets, where I passed Arab tea shops and ancient churches, rushed down along a dark covered street, or suddenly came upon a sunlit plaza, was a thrill. Being able to walk through all of Jerusalem was like waking from a nightmare. In one way that nightmare was the division of the city in 1948, which had prevented Jews from visiting the Wailing Wall. But in another that bad dream was the entire Jewish exile that we sang about every Passover. I did not want to move to Israel, but Jerusalem whole and united meant that the two thousand years of Jewish suffering were over.

Sari Nusseibeh was a philosophy student at Oxford University in 1968, but came home to East Jerusalem for the summer. Perhaps we passed each other on the streets of the Old City. But while I was in a dreamworld of hope, his emotions showed him a completely different place. "The Palestinian side of Jerusalem seemed moribund and uncertain of itself, just like me. It was neither under the boot of the Israeli military, like the West Bank, nor free, like the rest of Israel."

I wanted to see Israel's victory in the Six-Day War as a kind of magic, when, in fact, it was the product of hard battles in which men were killed and Palestinians lost control of the land where they lived. Surely, in 1968, I was too wide-eyed. But I was not alone in that initial fairy-dust hope followed by a queasy sense of disquiet. Because winning the Six-Day War did change everything.

In the Middle East, time runs backward. New wars are fought in order to alter the results of old wars. That is one big difference between here and there. Americans tend to be focused on the future; indeed, we are often criticized for having no sense of the past at all. Israelis and Palestinians argue about who lived where thousands of years ago, in order to define who should live where in the twenty-first century. This was certainly true in 1967. The Arabs were fighting to turn the clock back past 1956, past 1948, back to around 1914. In fact, even two months after the terrible defeats they suffered in the Six-Day War, Arab leaders proudly declared their three no's: "No recognition of Israel, no peace, and no negotiations with her." In other words they were behaving as if they had not just lost a war and as if Israel did not, could not, and should never exist.

And yet, while that was the stated policy of the Arabs, a shift did come after the 1967 war. The idea that the united Arab armies could drive the Jews into the sea was still often expressed—indeed, you hear that angry phrase to this day. But that goal became less and less a concrete aim of Arab policies. Even when Egypt and Syria attacked Israel in 1973, and did surprisingly well against the Israeli army, their goal was to recover land lost in 1967. Anwar Sadat, the very Egyptian leader who organized the 1973 war, then flew to Jerusalem in 1977 to personally end the conflict with Israel.

By winning so conclusively in 1967, Israel finally won the war of 1948. Israel proved to the Arabs that, at the least, the country was no easy target. As a state it was likely to survive. Indeed, in November of 1967, Israel, Egypt, and Jordan agreed to UN Resolution 242. While its language was crafted by diplomats and can be interpreted in many ways, the resolution basically implies that if Israel pulled back from land it had just conquered, the Arab states would stop trying to destroy Israel. (The diplomatic debates are about whether Israel needed to withdraw from all or just some of those conquered lands.) Sari Nusseibeh's father, Anwar, held meetings with King Hussein of Jordan, and with Israeli leaders such as Moshe Dayan and Golda Meir, trying to build from the baseline agreement in Resolution 242 into a peace treaty all could accept. But neither party could find a way to make that last step.

The basic acceptance of Israel represented by Resolution 242 meant that the first phase of Israel's history was over: The state had defended itself and was now on its feet; a reality. But Israel's very success now shifted the whole debate over the Middle East to the other issue left from 1948: the rights of the Palestinians. This was all the more true because Israel's victories meant that the Israeli government was directly responsible for more than one million Palestinians, as well as occupying their lands. Another two million Palestinians, who lived in refugee camps in Arab states, still had no citizenship, no hope, and no future.

Israelis saw this problem coming even while they fought the Six-Day War. How much land should Israel take, how much should it hold, how much should be used only as a bargaining chip on the road to peace? Those arguments began in 1967 and are still raging to this day. Why? Why didn't victory allow Israel to make the pragmatic deals needed to be free of conflict? Because in winning, Israel changed.

FROM SOCIALISM TO THE RED COW

As we have seen, the Zionists were not religious. Their goal was to create a semisocialist nation. This was not the Israel that the most Orthodox Jews believed God had promised them. So they turned against the modern state of Israel and continued to wait for the Messiah. Yet at the very moment that the Israelis took the Wailing Wall, the army's chief rabbi rushed to go there and pray. The new victories seemed like proof that God was leading the Jews back to all of their ancient lands. The time of the Messiah had come.

This argument was especially powerful because, so recently, millions of Jews had been murdered in the Holocaust. Why had that happened? Why had God brought so much suffering to the Jews? When the Israelis conquered the ancient lands of the Bible, some saw an answer. The terrible disaster of the Holocaust was a step on the way to the glorious coming of the Messiah. Now, Rabbi Zvi Yehuda Kook (whose father and my grandfather had been leading rabbis in Palestine at the same time), declared that Jews must settle the West Bank, the ancient lands of Judea and Samaria. In other words, the West Bank was not occupied land that belonged to the Palestinians who lived there. Instead God was giving the land to the Jews, which they must settle to fulfill His commandments.

This kind of thinking is the opposite of rational modern Zionism. The closest parallel is the beliefs of Evangelical Protestants in America, who are against teaching evolution and against embryonic stem-cell research, and who believe God intends America to save the world. In fact, some of those Evangelicals actually agree with the Jews who saw the 1967 war as a sign that we are very near the end of human history. According to an ancient Jewish law, a red cow—a perfectly red cow, with no more than two black hairs and no white hairs—is needed as part of a purification ceremony that must take place when the Messiah comes. Christian cattle breeders in Texas have worked with Jewish rabbis to breed such a red cow. But how is it that Israel, whose founding ideal was the socialist kibbutz, could swing so far away from reason and toward faith?

Imagine if the Palestinians had managed to take back parts of Israel in 1967. Surely upon seeing their villages they would have felt similar emotions—belonging, return, a sense of being blessed by Allah. Those are just human feelings that anyone might experience on regaining long-lost lands, especially if these are places you and your relatives have talked, and prayed, and read about for thousands of years. Had the Palestinians taken those villages, surely no one could have convinced them that some of the land should be given up again, even if that could bring peace.

As a gut feeling, the sentiment in Israel in favor of holding conquered territories was natural and understandable, very much like my own sense of magic while walking through the Old City of Jerusalem. Even Kook's message might have been just a curiosity, like the various predictions for the date on which Jesus will return, which Christian groups in America have seen come and go. But the matter of the occupied lands did not remain an emotion or a biblical prophecy. For Jews began to move across the old borders of their state, into the conquered territories, and to build settlements. They were announcing with their concrete and roads and guns that this land belonged to them.

THE BROTHERS

At some point any book on Israel talks about the sabra, the prickly pear. Native-born Israelis have long seen themselves as being like that fruit: bristling with spikes on the outside, warm and sweet on the inside. If you know an Israeli Jew, you can easily see why the image fits. But recently I've heard people suggest that the image should be reversed: Israelis claim to be nice, moderate, and reasonable, while they are actually brutal. These critics are thinking of the West Bank settlers, Jews who can be as barbaric as the American pioneers who ran Indians off of their land, yet who, like those Americans, speak of themselves as civilized, humane, and of those they abuse as savages. Rather than debating which version of the sabra fits, another new image seems more appropriate to me: I see the Israeli Jews and the Palestinians in the occupied territories as Siamese twins attached back-to-back.

From 1948 to 1967, each twin faced only his own world, ignoring the tugs he felt from time to time. The Jews were entirely focused on building their nation, their homeland. Palestinians were essentially invisible to them. Golda Meir summed that view up perfectly, saying "it was not as though there was a Palestinian people in Palestine considering itself a Palestinian people and we came and threw them out and took their country away from them. They did not exist." But the Palestinians were just as blind to the Israeli Jews. Taken with Nasser's idea of joining with all of the Arab peoples, they agreed that Israel could not, should not, and would not exist. The two brothers were attached, but not only did they believe they were separate, they did not even accept that the other was there at all.

When the Israelis took over East Jerusalem and the West Bank, the brothers began to become visible to each other, and neither liked what they saw. Realizing that they were actually attached to Palestinians made some Israeli Jews want to cleanse their land, to banish all non-Jews, while to others the visible presence of the Palestinians showed that their idealistic nation rested on the suffering of another brutalized people. In turn, realizing that the Jews were there for good made some Palestinians all the more violent and desperate, while it taught others that they needed to learn from the Jews. They could not just merge into the Arab world; they needed create a state of their own.

The word "settlement" harkens back to the early days of Israel; it suggests pioneering. The Jews moving into the West Bank could feel as if they were their own grandparents, repeating the same story of carving a modern state out of the ancient Promised Land. The trouble was that this was land owned and inhabited by Palestinians with nowhere else to go. If Jews were reliving the founding of Israel by moving to the West Bank, they were defining their nation as a conquering state that had no interest in any legal or human rights—only the rights of guns, and the supposed will of God. If Palestinians were seeing the "catastrophe" of 1948 being replayed, they now knew that the greater Arab world would not wipe Israel away. They were on their own.

Jewish settlement in the occupied lands of the West Bank was a rerun of the founding of Israel, except this time in a moral environment in which international support for Israel itself had changed the rules: The rights of minorities must now be protected. Israel was both a conqueror like any other—as the World War I winners had been fifty years earlier—and a state created to protect the rights of the victims of discrimination and prejudice. The Jews of Israel knew that they could not just evict the Palestinians. Or, to be more precise, some Jews did. Others had no qualms at all about redrawing borders and pushing out Palestinians.

The big issue I keep mentioning—the rights you gain by winning versus the moral rights that belong to all people as human beings—played out as a divide within Israel itself over what to do with the occupied lands. The settlers garnered powerful support. Their cause was taken up by rising political parties, which represented a major shift in Israel's population. That is one part of what many people speak of as the hardening of Israel, the poisoning that came with victory in 1967.

THE OTHER JEWS IN ISRAEL

As I mentioned earlier, the very image of progressive, modern Israel was the socialist kibbutz. But not only were the kibbutzniks a small minority of the Jews, they were almost entirely European Jews. We were eating pickled herring for breakfast in Galilee because that is what the older generation of kibbutz members had grown up eating back in Poland. The Mizrahi Jews, who came to Israel in the late 1940s and '50s from the rest of the world, had no desire to join the kibbutzim, nor did the kibbutzim make any effort to recruit them. By the 1970s, the kibbutz was no longer a symbol of Israel but of the divisions within the country.

Ben-Gurion once described the North African Jew this way: He "looks like a savage"; he "never read a book in his life, not even a religious one, and doesn't even know how to say his prayers." This disdain on the part of the Ashkenazi socialist founders only made the Mizrahi Jews feel dead set against the policies of Israel's ruling elite. The European-educated leadership was considering how to make the best rational deal: trading what they called the West Bank to the Arabs in exchange for greater security for Israel. The Mizrahis were determined to keep what they called the biblical kingdoms of Judea and Samaria and to meet Arab threats with more aggressive Israeli tactics.

By the 1970s, the Mizrahis amounted to about half of Israel's Jewish population. In 1977, Menachem Begin, who had moved far away from his youthful terrorism, courted them. Rather than seeing the kibbutzim as the heart of Israel, he called them rich, indulged, and irrelevant. Riding on the wave of Mizrahi votes, he was elected prime minister of Israel.

In the ten years since the 1967 war, eighty settlements were built in the conquered lands of the Jordan's west bank, filled with about eleven thousand Jews. Today, there are 125 official settlements, which 250,000 Jews claim as their homes. That shift from a trickle of settlers to the modern flood tide began with Begin's election.

Begin did not speak of the West Bank or the occupied territories. Instead he used the biblical names Judea and Samaria, and he was determined to fill the lands that had belonged to Jews thousands of years ago with new Jewish settlers. Begin was not apologetic. He did not care about trampling on the rights of Palestinians, or that moderate allies of Israel might disapprove. In his mind, Jews had every right to settle land they had conquered, land that God had promised them

OPPOSITE PAGE: *Even map labels are controversial when they describe places Israel conquered in 1967. We use "West Bank" as a geographical term because the precise boundaries of the Palestinian state that will take shape in that area have not been settled.*

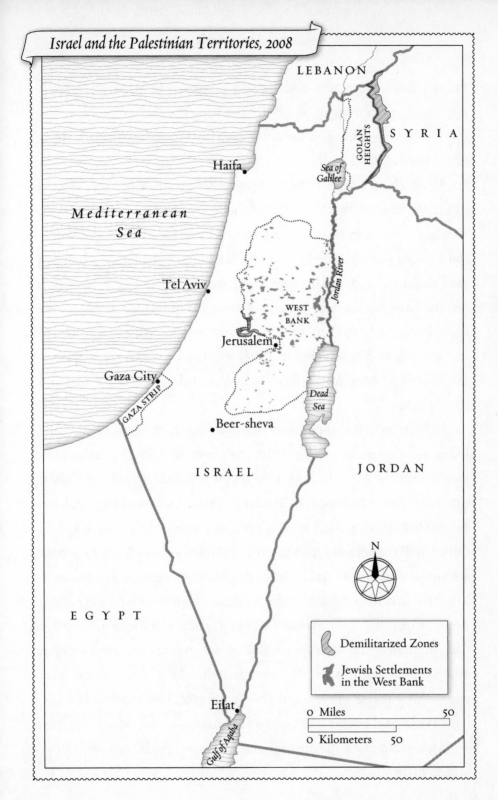

Israel and the Palestinian Territories, 2008

LEBANON

SYRIA

Haifa

Mediterranean Sea

Sea of Galilee

GOLAN HEIGHTS

Jordan River

Tel Aviv

WEST BANK

Jerusalem

Gaza City

GAZA STRIP

Dead Sea

Beer-sheva

ISRAEL

JORDAN

EGYPT

N

Eilat

Gulf of Aqaba

Demilitarized Zones

Jewish Settlements in the West Bank

0 Miles   50

0 Kilometers   50

III

thousands of years ago, with Jewish homes, schools, streets, walls, guns, and swimming pools. Both the religious believers expecting the Messiah to come and the Mizrahis eager to see a stronger, larger Israel were pleased.

Again, there is a good American parallel. Andrew Jackson, elected president in 1828, was the voice of the West—the rough-hewn, back-woods, do-it-yourself Americans who had previously been ignored by the Eastern elite. You feel the swell of democracy in action when you read about Jackson and his rowdy supporters arriving in Washington. But the Eastern elite had spoken for the rights of Indians and included abolitionists determined to end slavery. In the same way, the old European Jewish leadership in Israel was talking about trading lands taken in 1967 back to the Palestinians, in order to bring a final and lasting peace.

Jackson and his supporters were totally unsympathetic to the Indians they fought or the slaves they owned. Like the Jacksonian Democrats, the Mizrahi Jews were tough-minded, prejudiced against those of different ethnicities, and angry at the snobbish but moralistic ruling elite. Having lived in Muslim countries until they were kicked out or fled, the Mizrahi Jews felt they understood the Arabs as people who respected toughness and power, not negotiation and compromise. The Mizrahis were against giving back any land or trusting any Arab promise of peace. Just as Israel debated what to do with the land it had conquered, the Mizrahi Jews came out in force to vote for Begin and against compromise. The very fact that Israel was a democracy was making it less open-minded, less rational, less and less like the land Willie and people like him had labored to build.

Back in America, the liberal Judaism I grew up with was also under attack, from all sides.

THE OTHER JEWS IN AMERICA

At every Passover meal I've been to, people are careful to be inclusive. While the Passover ceremony recounts the story of Moses and the Jews escaping from slavery in Egypt, someone is sure to mention other peoples who are still enduring captivity and oppression. Some households even include the Palestinians. But in the 1960s the most obvious group to include were American blacks, involved in their struggle for civil rights. Jewish college students, Jewish rabbis, Jewish lawyers eagerly joined the cause. That was the world I lived in, a world in which the civil rights movement was goodness itself. Andrew Goodman, who was killed in Mississippi in 1964 working for black rights, had gone to school across the street from me. He stood for all of us, Jews who felt the cause of civil rights might even be worth risking our lives. To be Jewish, as I understood it, was to be for black rights. Jackie Robinson's visit to my school was one of the great moments of my childhood, and I still remember shaking his strong, calloused hand.

Just about the time of the Six-Day War, the civil rights movement began to fracture. Advocates of black power were not interested in Jewish allies. Indeed, they loudly shouted out for separation, or even revolution, declaring that blacks needed to stay true to their communities and roots, and to reject all of white society. The black nationalists, with their talk of guns and war in the streets, scared me. But I also felt excluded, shut out. And while Jews like me no longer knew where we fit in the black liberation struggle, some black revolutionaries found common cause with the Palestinians.

THE PLO

When the PLO was established in 1964, the group was not an important player in the Middle East conflict. In fact, it was designed merely
to echo the views and plans that came from Nasser and other leaders
of large Arab nations. Yasir Arafat took over the leadership of the
PLO in 1969, and he totally changed the organization. Arafat was
the kind of firebrand who, in another time, would have led a clan of
warriors on horseback from one victory to another. He inspired the
Palestinians to feel that they were a people, that they had rights, and
that they could rise. Defeated by the Israelis, manipulated by their
Arab allies, the Palestinians found a voice in Arafat. The problem was
that while Arafat could ignite the Palestinians, he could not make any
productive use of that flame.

Arafat's leadership was deeply flawed. Even people who worked
closely with him, such as Sari Nusseibeh, say he was fearful to the
point of paranoia; obsessed with monopolizing all power, and thus all
funds, for himself and his cronies; often out of touch with ordinary
Palestinians; and given to making terrible decisions, such as publicly
supporting Saddam Hussein in the first Gulf War. He could speak
for Palestinian anger, but could not guide Palestinians toward pragmatic choices that would improve their lives. The well-spoken Israeli
politician and author Abba Eban captured Arafat's many mistakes in
judgment with a perfect phrase: The PLO leader "never missed an
opportunity to miss an opportunity."

Arafat did, though, make one crucial step. With his rise, the Palestinians, now living in land occupied by the Israelis, began to realize
that they needed to have a state of their own. In other words, they
could no longer just dream of turning back the clock. The Palestinians

needed to see themselves as a distinct people and to create a nation; they needed to become like the Israelis. Arafat helped the Palestinians to recognize that they were attached back-to-back with the Israelis, and so needed to detach, and stand alone.

Arafat made the Palestinians the center of the conflict, and linked their struggle against the Jews to other national liberation movements around the world. Arafat claimed that the Palestinians were like blacks in America or South Africa, yet another group of victims whose rights were being trampled. This argument appealed to some blacks and leftists in America, Europe, Africa, and the Caribbean.

The fact that Arafat spoke of liberation was not in itself special. Nasser and others had also claimed that they were fighting for the oppressed peoples of the world. When it became clear that Egypt's armies were being crushed during the Six-Day War, Nasser spread the lie that Israel was being helped by America and England, which led to anti-American riots throughout the Arab world.

Today we associate anti-American feeling among Arabs with religion, as if the conflict were between Islam and the largely Christian West. But Nasser persecuted Muslim leaders and was antireligious, and yet he used the same language. Attacking America and Israel was a way to rile people up—to create a demon and to deflect blame. Arafat's talk by itself did not make the cause of the Palestinians more persuasive. But the more the issue in the Middle East shifted from Arab states wanting to destroy Israel, to Palestinian people claiming a right to live in peace—with dignity, in their own land—the more conflict this created for some American Jews.

You didn't have to believe a single word Arafat said to be disturbed by the increasing talk of a "Greater Israel" in which the Jews would keep all of the West Bank and the Palestinians had no place at all. The magic of a united Jerusalem began to look more like an illusion and a curse, for it turned the Israel that liberal Jews, like me, admired into the image of everything evil in the world. If we read Thoreau, favored black rights, were against the war in Vietnam, and saw South African defenders of apartheid as racists, how could we defend Israel for not only holding Palestinian lands but filling them with new Jewish settlements? And as we struggled to make sense of this, a new voice began to be heard among American Jews.

Even as the black separatists were telling Jews they didn't want our help, some Jews began to speak of "Jewish Pride." Enough with trying to save other people, they said, what about *our* community, *our* roots? Don't try to blend in with other Americans, don't be afraid to be Jewish. The Jewish Defense League, founded in 1968 by a Brooklyn lawyer named Meir Kahane, encouraged Jews to arm themselves with guns and to be ready to fight. Kahane later moved to Israel, where he was such a dangerous and violent advocate of Jewish settlement that his political party was finally banned.

The rise of what you might call the tough Jews in America came just as the mood in Israel was changing. In fact, they made a perfect fit. Some of the Jews in America who turned more religious were inspired by the idea that the conquered territories had been given to Jews by God. Indeed, American Jews began to move to Israel, to live in new settlements on the West Bank. Other Jews, who did not accept the religious argument, still felt a bond with Begin and the Mizrahi Jews. They saw the old socialist Zionism as similar to the old liberal Jewish devotion to civil rights. Both were elite ideals that had little to do with the realities of a hard, tough world in which every person and every group had to watch out for itself.

The capstone to this time of transition came in the 1980s when hippies turned into yuppies. Making money and buying expensive toys took the place of living in communes and marching for causes. This same spirit reached Israel, where the whole kibbutz movement teetered on the edge of bankruptcy. As one sad Israeli put it, instead of working for the good of all, you got busy "taking care of number one." Settlers rushing to live in nice homes on occupied lands were like the children who said good-bye to their parents' kibbutzim and went off to get MBAs or to work for companies in Silicon Valley.

Winning the Six-Day War showed Israel's strength. But deciding what to do with the territories split Israel into two camps, pitting the European Zionists with their old ideals against the newly confident Mizrahi Jews, religious Jews, and tough conservative Jews. Those divisions in Israel only deepened in the next decades, as new wars alternated with new peace initiatives. While the Six-Day War has not led to a civil war, as the Mexican War did in America, it might. Each new round of conflict with the Palestinians reopened the same increasingly important question: Can Israel occupy conquered land, defend itself against the anger of the defeated, build new settlements, and still remain true to its highest ideals?

IV. Can Israel Occupy Conquered Lands and Be True to Its Ideals?

UPRISING

Let's start outside Israel and the occupied lands, with Lebanon in 1982. At that time the PLO had not accepted UN Resolution 242, and was committed to the destruction of Israel. Indeed, terrorists from the Palestinian Black September movement had murdered eleven Israeli athletes at the 1972 Olympics. The term "Black September" actually had nothing to do with Israel. Rather, the name referred to the clash in September of 1970, when the PLO tried to prevent Jordan from cooperating in any peace plans. In effect, the PLO attempted to take over Jordan itself, but King Hussein defeated Arafat and his men, and threw them out of the country. The PLO, the organization dedicated to the "liberation" of Palestine, was forced to relocate to Beirut. Lebanon is on Israel's northern border, and the PLO began a new round of attacks.

Lebanon itself was, and is, a deeply divided country, and the PLO's presence helped spark a civil war between Christians and Muslims. In 1981, Ariel Sharon was Israel's defense minister, and he argued that Israel needed to be a kind of dentist, cleaning the infection of PLO fighters out of Lebanon, which would also help the Christians in their battle for control of the country. He was given permission to go a short way into Lebanon, just enough to make Israel more secure. But when Sharon led his forces into Lebanon, they went well beyond the agreed line. Not only did they march all the way to the capital city of Beirut, they provided the illumination at night that allowed Christians to enter the Sabra and Shatila Palestinian refugee camps and murder some seven or eight hundred civilians. Although the Israelis finally stopped the bloodshed, the slaughter could not have taken place without their help.

The massacre at the refugee camps sickened many Israelis. Indeed, some four hundred thousand people, nearly 10 percent of the country, rallied to demand the investigation and prosecution of those responsible for the deaths.

Israel had every right to defend itself against the PLO, which was, at the time, a terrorist organization using Lebanon as a base to harm Israelis. But in doing so, Israel assisted in the murder of innocent people. The Israeli revulsion against the massacres showed the soft side of the sabra, the heart. But the Israeli soldiers who went into Lebanon were fighting a different war from the battles of '48, '56, '67, or '73. This was a harsher, dirtier fight. Instead of uniformed soldiers battling with a kind of discipline and honor against other professionals, soldiers had to go from house to house. Terrorists used civilians as shields, so soldiers sometimes killed women or mangled children. And how could you tell who was a terrorist? Soldiers needed to interrogate prisoners—and to decide how much torture was acceptable to pry out information that might save Israeli lives. Like Americans who fought in Vietnam, Israelis were being hardened by their own actions. An Israeli who suffered from nightmares, flashbacks, and insomnia after the Lebanon War said that he and his fellow soldiers were "amputees of the soul." They had lost that spark of humanity and life.

And for what? Although Sharon resigned as defense minister because of the outrage over the massacre he oversaw, he remained a popular politician. When the PLO left Lebanon, a new terrorist organization, called Hezbollah, took its place. Hezbollah is tougher, better armed, and—because the group has the support of Iran—a much more dangerous enemy than the old PLO. Sharon's invasion accomplished nothing.

While the massacres in Lebanon shocked Israelis, the campaign itself was short. The real price of the occupation became clear in 1987 and 1988. It was in 1987 when the first Intifada, which can mean "shaking off" or "uprising," began in the West Bank. By then, any Palestinian under the age of twenty was the child of a refugee and had lived his or her entire life as a refugee. What horizon of hope did they have? The old idea that Arab armies would sweep Israel away was appealing as a fantasy, but seemed increasingly unreal. And every day the Palestinians were questioned by Israeli soldiers, stopped at Israeli checkpoints, or were ordered around by Israeli officers telling them where they could or could not go. Feeling entirely hemmed in, Palestinian young men turned to violence—often as not throwing stones.

The first Intifada completely changed Sari Nusseibeh. A graduate of Oxford and Harvard, he sounds, in his memoir, like an American college professor. He loves reading old books and weighing their philosophical ideas. When in America, he was most drawn to visit Monticello, because Thomas Jefferson was so important to him. Sari knew full well about Jefferson's terrible record on slavery, but he still treasured Jefferson's deep love for liberty and freedom. The Lemon Tree Café, which Sari ran in Old Jerusalem, was an oasis of conversation, where liberal Israeli Jews would drink coffee late into the night, trading opinions with similar Palestinian thinkers. The place sounds so appealing, I feel as if I've been there—or should have had I known about it.

During the first Intifada, Sari became the secret nerve center of the uprising—spreading news, passing information, crystallizing the proposals and demands of the Palestinians. He was always playing cat and mouse with the Israelis, who were determined to shut down that information flow. Why would this thoughtful philosopher—who had once lived on a kibbutz in Israel and continued to have close Israeli friends, this family man who cared most for his wife and children—not only support the rock-throwing uprising that was putting so many young Palestinians at risk of jail, interrogation, even death, but make it his life's cause?

In a sense, Sari was like the boy who notices that the emperor has no clothes. He realized that the Israelis and the Palestinians were fooling themselves: both knew what the future had to be—some version of that old Peel Plan in which the land was divided into two distinct states. But this meant an admission neither side was willing to state out loud. Palestinians knew that in order to have their own state, they would have to accept the loss of their lands from 1948 and build on the territory in which they now lived. Taking that step meant breaking ranks with other Arabs, and finally and fully accepting Israel. Israeli Jews knew that they could not remain occupiers forever, and that the one million Palestinians in the West Bank needed better lives, but to say that was to admit that the Palestinians existed and deserved a state of their own. What both sides knew, neither would admit.

Sari came to believe that precisely because the Israeli leadership knew what must eventually happen, they were doing everything to drive the Palestinians toward greater violence, to discourage the growth of strong nonviolent leadership. He felt Israelis were constantly trying to provoke the Palestinians, who readily took the bait, thus allowing the Israelis to delay granting the Palestinians a state, and, instead, to build more settlements, to claim more land.

What could be done to break this chain of violence and deception? Sari felt that the Palestinians needed to assert that Golda Meir was wrong—the Palestinians did exist as a people; they were not invisible; they were not to be swept aside by settlers, and they needed to be heard. Sari favored only nonviolent protest; he did not support bombings and murder, but he also thought action, assertion, was necessary. He saw his college students grow, even from the process of being arrested by the Israelis and put in jail; they gained a sense of their own freedom by protesting against the Israeli occupation. Something similar was true of the early civil rights protesters in the American South. Their victory was in taking the risk to speak out. After that, whether or not they were arrested or jailed, did not matter. They found their voice by speaking.

While the Palestinians found themselves in action and in protest, Israeli Jews began to feel that they were losing themselves by imprisoning and interrogating the Palestinians.

When soldiers anywhere need to contain violent young men, they do whatever is necessary to protect themselves and do their jobs. Sometimes they follow the nice rules for military behavior that are set down in codes of law. Sometimes they don't. Faced with an angry, violent uprising, Israeli soldiers toughened, as had the soldiers in Lebanon. To use a very recent American parallel, during the second Iraq War, American soldiers humiliated and tortured Iraqi prisoners in Abu Ghraib prison. Imagine that America had experienced terrorist attacks not just on September 11, 2001, but over and over again, and imagine that it faced an enemy close at hand, not thousands of miles away. I am sure there might well be far more Abu Ghraibs. (To this day, concerned people within and outside of the American military debate whether the abuse of prisoners was a result of rogue soldiers under stress, or policy decisions by higher officers.)

In the way that the Middle East always looks backward, the Intifada replayed the Great Revolt of the 1930s. To this day, the rockets that anti-Israeli forces lob into the country almost daily are named Qassams, after that hero of the fight against the Jews (see page 43). In turn, Israeli leaders who grew up reading about how the British had put down the Great Revolt tried to use precisely the same harsh techniques to end the Intifada.

The Israelis used cruel and illegal methods against Palestinians. For example, they deprived suspected insurgents of sleep or food, and threatened them physically and emotionally. (These are similar to techniques that the American CIA has used against suspected terrorists after 9/11, and which are now coming under legal and congressional criticism.) When a Palestinian attacker was caught, his home might be destroyed, leaving his entire family homeless. During the first Intifada some two thousand homes were bulldozed, approximately one thousand Palestinians were killed by Israelis, and another eighteen thousand were injured. As many as one hundred seventy-five thousand were jailed, of which some twenty-three thousand were treated so harshly that the word "torture" would be appropriate.

Earlier in this book, I mentioned Jeffrey Goldberg, the writer from Long Island. Unlike me, he decided to move to Israel. Even today, as a reporter, he is a risk taker. He puts himself in danger often, going after stories certain to test his courage, and he was eager to serve in the Israeli army. After college he exercised his "right of return," moved to Israel, and joined the army. Goldberg was assigned to be a guard at Ketziot, the large prison Israel built to house the many Palestinians being jailed during the first Intifada.

If you have ever seen a prison movie, you know that no matter how strict the facility, the inmates try to find ways to bend the rules. At Ketziot, for example, one book from the prison library was a surprising favorite: the autobiography of Menachem Begin. Why? Because Begin had been a terrorist fighting against the British; his example inspired the Palestinians in their clash with Israel. The Palestinians also discovered a new use for rock throwing. In the prison, they used pebbles to toss messages from one cell to another. But one day, a whizzing pebble with a message hit an Israeli Jew. That was really bad. It looked as if the prisoners were rebelling, turning to violence against their guards.

One of the Palestinian prison leaders let Goldberg know that the pebble had not been intended as a weapon. Jeff didn't think he was lying. But his commanding officer was not about to let the violation pass.

"Take a prisoner to solitary confinement," the officer ordered.

"Which prisoner?"

"Any prisoner."

You cannot just force an innocent person into solitary because someone threw a pebble. Well, you can, but it is not legal, it is not right. "I couldn't do it," Jeff thought. "It was un-American."

At that moment, in that prison, he began to realize that he was fundamentally American. He saw that the basic ideas of human rights he had been taught were not trumped by a prison filled with Palestinians—many of whom actually did believe in destroying Israel and killing Jews—or even by his sworn obligation to defend Israel.

Jeff's story highlights the issues that have come up throughout this book: Is Israel a tribe, a clan, held together by being Jewish, or is it a nation, bound by laws that apply to all? Does safety come by being with people like you, or by being equally fair to everyone? I believe that Israel is in danger of becoming a fortress of Judaism, not an expression of Jewish values. Being occupiers and settlers hardens Israeli Jews, which then makes them all the less capable of relating to Arab Israelis—and that undermines Israel itself.

The abuses on the Israeli side do not mean that the Palestinians themselves had any interest in human rights. During the Intifada, they killed five hundred of their own people, either because of disputes between different factions, or because the victims were suspected of collaborating with the Israelis. Indeed, the Palestinians chose to keep throwing stones, even as their violence destroyed their economy and endangered their families. Sari watched as his students shifted from finding a sense of freedom and dignity in their protests to becoming ever more hardened, silent, and committed to violence.

The Israelis did what they believed they had to do to protect themselves. The Palestinians did what they believed they had to do to assert themselves. They brutalized one another, and in turn, made themselves more brutal.

For Israelis who truly believe their nation has a moral mission, who believe Zionism is about making a better country, and who shared the ideals of the old kibbutzniks, to see Jews involved in massacres, in torture, is the most terrible nightmare. To the credit of the Israelis, these idealists have not kept quiet. They constantly press their nation to face its crimes and its failings. Some six hundred Israelis refused to serve in the territories during the first Intifada.

Willie's son, Gideon, is a sabra, a Zionist who grew up on his father's kibbutz, and was injured in the war in 1973. Gidi says that controlling the West Bank has made the Israelis "rough inside." Dov Yirma, who fought for Israel in 1948, agrees. "We've shown in many ways that we are no better than anyone else. In the Zionist movement, they wanted a new sort of secular Jew in an idealistic nation of justice, mercy, and well-being. That was the basis of kibbutz thought, and this has failed."

Sometimes I think the problem is those high moral expectations for Israel, and for America. Why can't our countries just admit that we are pragmatic realists who do whatever serves our national interests? Israel exists because it has an army, nuclear weapons, and American support. It has no obligation to be "fair" to the Palestinians, only to treat them in whatever way is most likely to make Israel more secure. Russians are not "fair" to Chechens. The Chinese are not "fair" to Tibetans. Syria, which experts believe has had its hand in a string of assassinations, is not "fair" to Lebanon. Neither Indians nor Pakistanis are "fair" to the people of Kashmir. Of all of the Arab nations holding Palestinian refugees, only Jordan has been even minimally "fair." And yet when you listen to Israelis themselves, you hear their need to be something more than just another bully in a world of bullies. They need Israel to mean something, and yearn to live in a nation that has kept its human face.

Roni Hirschenson lost one son to a suicide bomber. Another son was a soldier whose best friend was the first Israeli killed in the Intifada. Three weeks later Roni's son killed himself. "I don't want even my enemy to share this pain," Roni says. "No human being deserves this." He has devoted his life to a group called the Families Forum. Half of the members are Israeli, half are Palestinian. All have lost family members to the fighting.

Mr. Hirschenson shows how Israelis and Palestinians can use

their will and determination, not only to build nations, but to remain human in the face of terrible pain. They—not the settlers eager to take over more Palestinian land, not the radicals who stir up Palestinian hatred—are the true idealists. But it is too much to ask parents who have lost their children to be the conscience of the nation.

WHY DO THESE CONFLICTS CONTINUE?

By the end of 1988, the first Intifada showed the Palestinians that stones alone would do no good, and Arafat realized he needed to make some move toward Israel. In turn, a majority of Israelis accepted that the occupation could not continue forever. Ehud Barak, the most decorated soldier in Israel's history, and later its prime minister, said the Intifada was a sign that the Israeli occupation could not go on. "It was a misjudgment of reality to believe that a Jewish state could rule over another people for twenty years."

In December, Arafat accepted UN Resolution 242, although interpreting it to mean that all of the Israeli settlements in the West Bank and the Gaza Strip would be removed. Four years later, after many public and secret talks, Arafat and Israel's Prime Minister Yitzhak Rabin signed an agreement outlining the steps toward peace. The Palestinian Authority, as it was now called, took over governing the Palestinian people. At the time, it seemed that both sides had had enough of the poison. So it seemed.

CHOOSING GOD OVER PEACE

On November 4, 1995, Yitzak Rabin, having now signed a second agreement with Arafat, came to a large rally in Tel Aviv. In exactly six months the two leaders were to meet again to resolve the final details on the deal that would give Palestinians a homeland, and guarantee Israel's safety. Some 150,000 Israelis gathered to cheer him. One did not. For months the most extreme rabbis had been preaching against Rabin, condemning him for giving away the very land that they believed God had promised the Jews, apparently undoing the miracle of 1967. The rabbis harangued, screamed, used the most violent language. Their followers listened. Yigal Amir, a twenty-five-year-old religious student, pulled out a gun and murdered Rabin.

The religious Jews who saw the taking of Judea and Samaria as a sign that the Messiah was about to appear had no interest in negotiated settlements. For them, there was no peace process. They were concerned with red cows and prophecies. They were not worried about the damage to their sons' "human face" from having to patrol amid the Palestinians. Amir assassinated Rabin so that he would not "give our country to the Arabs."

Rabin was a kind of Abraham Lincoln, taking the risk of leading his country toward where it needed to go. For Lincoln that meant ending slavery, re-dedicating America to a larger vision of "liberty and justice" that truly applied to "all." He paid with his life. Rabin too was taking Israel toward the only rational future it could have, and he met the same fate.

Arafat was not a devout Muslim. During the Intifada, though, two Islamic groups began to gain followers among the Palestinians: Hamas and Islamic Jihad. Like the Orthodox rabbis in Israel, they were not interested in negotiated settlements nor did they want to get a better deal for the Palestinians. On the one hand, Hamas provided services for the Palestinians that the PLO, for all of its fine words, did not. Hamas filled a true need in Palestinian society by setting up charities, hospitals, schools, and libraries. On the other hand, Hamas wanted the Palestinians to become devout Muslims, and to destroy Israel.

Hamas and Islamic Jihad brought to Israel a tactic also used by Hezbollah, based in Lebanon: the suicide bomber. Terrorism spread from the occupied territories into the heart of Jerusalem and Haifa and Tel Aviv, and—because it lies at Israel's narrowest point—the seacoast city of Netanya, where a good number of my relatives live.

Whether it was Yigal Amir assassinating the prime minister who agreed to give land back to the Palestinians, or Hamas preaching Muslim fundamentalism and sending human bombs to kill civilians, religious extremists on both sides did their best to end the process of negotiation and compromise. They succeeded. But the full measure of their success did not become clear until 2000. That year, Israel's Prime Minister Ehud Barak made one big, all-out, effort to reach final peace with Arafat. Not only did he fail, but the second Intifada that soon followed has left both sides so hardened and grim that the Israelis have built a physical wall to make sure they stay apart. You can actually see the concrete barrier that the Israelis built to seal themselves in (or keep the Palestinians out).

LIGHTNING

"Barak" means "lightning" in Hebrew, and the prime minister made his reputation through his courage and decisiveness as a soldier. His effort to settle the entire Israel–Palestine issue all at once was another form of lightning strike. Barak's gamble was the essence of everything Israel had been back to the days of the Zionist pioneers: bold, risk-taking, aimed at creating a nation (actually two: Israel and Palestine). Barak even spoke about giving back part of Jerusalem, a subject no

Israeli leader had ever mentioned in public. This was as good an offer as Arafat would ever get. But that is what it was, a pragmatic deal in which Barak wanted the best for Israel, and enough for the Palestinians to allow them to agree.

Arafat said no.

Picture a schoolyard fight in which two boys have bloodied each other and their friends are trying to pull them apart. To end the combat, each just has to mumble enough of an apology to allow the other to keep his pride and walk away. Both of the fighters know what they have to do and are measuring how to look tough, not give an inch, but say something. "You go first," one spits out, "you started it." "You first," the other snarls back, "you hit me." In an instant they are at it again, punches flying, and the fight ignites once more, this time over who should be first to apologize for starting the old fight. In a sense that is what happened between Barak and Arafat.

Ever since Arafat and Rabin made their agreement, the Palestinians felt cheated by the Israelis. The Israelis have used two tactics over and over again in their negotiations: They demand much more than they expect to get, so that as they have to haggle and trade, they have plenty to give away and still wind up ahead; and they come into negotiations having created "facts on the ground" that favor them. The more well-established settlements that were building up homes, walls, and swimming pools in the West Bank, the more pieces Israel had to trade, and the stronger its argument for the need to keep some of that conquered land in the final agreement. These strategies made the Palestinians furious. Here they had accepted Israel's right to exist (more or less); they had given away their biggest bargaining chip, and they had nothing to show for it but the steady drone of concrete being poured, roads being built, the occupied territories becoming more and more Jewish. "Stop the settlements," the Palestinians said. "Prove your good intentions, then we can have peace." You go first.

The Israeli Jews, in turn, were furious at the Palestinians. Arafat never showed either the will or the ability to stop the suicide bombings, or to prevent terrorism. And every so often there would be a sign that the Palestinian acceptance of Israel was, at best, provisional, such as the materials used to teach Palestinian children that included maps on which Israel did not exist. "Stop the terrorism and propaganda," the Jews said. "We did our part by accepting that there will be a Palestinian state, now prove your good intentions. Then we can have peace." You go first.

Israeli Jews behave like an imperiled minority that must hold on to any tiny bit of land or security it has gained. They point to the size of the Arab armies, the ferocity of the Palestinian attacks, the anti-Semitic slurs that still openly circulate in the Palestinian, Arab, and Muslim worlds. Although their nation is sixty years old, and was founded on the idea of creating the new, strong, Jew, the Israelis act as if they are still fragile immigrants who must clutch and cling to all they possess. The Palestinians portray themselves as being crushed under the heel of the Israeli police. They see Israel as backed by America, the world's only superpower, and themselves as people without a state, a homeland, or basic human rights. They feel they have lost everything, so they cannot give anything more.

Which is the strong party that can afford to be generous and which is the weak party that must be supported, have its hand held through danger? In fact, each side nurses its own pains and grievances. Yet those who have lost the most, like those Jewish and Palestinian parents in the Families Forum, keep telling us that we must recognize the other's pain to gain solace for our own.

In 2000, I thought Barak was right and Arafat wrong. But maybe Barak was being too Israeli. Israelis know how to build a nation. I suspect that if Arafat had asked for help in building his Palestinian state, Barak would have been eager to offer assistance, like the old socialists on the kibbutzim, waiting for the Arab farmers to come and ask for guidance. Yet perhaps all the Palestinians could see was the suffering they had experienced and the ruin around them. How could all of that add up to just fragments of territory on a map? Somehow Barak would have had to be as understanding as he was bold. Or Arafat needed to be a Lincoln, a Rabin, a Gandhi who would lead his people beyond their passions, even at the risk of his own life. But neither was that kind of leader. The talks failed.

At that moment many Israelis of good will, including most of my relatives, gave up. If the Palestinians could not accept a deal that gave them a nation, what could they possibly want except to destroy Israel? Building a nation means everything to those Israelis. How could the Palestinians have refused that opportunity? Anyone who has been in a fight knows that the urge to destroy everything, especially if you are hurting, is much more powerful than the abstract idea of swallowing your pride and starting over. The Palestinians also gave up on talking.

When the same Ariel Sharon, who had gone into Lebanon, marched toward the Dome of the Rock in Jerusalem flanked by sup-porters, he was being deliberately provocative, but he was probably doing so mainly in order to impress those tough Mizrahi Israeli voters. The Palestinians used the incident as an excuse to start a second Intifada, only this time not with rocks but with suicide bombs. Soon enough the al-Aqsa Martyrs Brigade, a faction that the Israelis (and other outside observers) claim was allied with Arafat, also turned to the human guided missile.

V. How Can Israel Be a Strong State, a Jewish Homeland, and Truly Democratic?

"LET NO ONE SAY HE DID NOT KNOW"

Right here I could write a section similar to the one about the first Intifada. I could fill it with moving diary entries teenagers wrote just before they were blown up by suicide bombs; or with the aching words of parents such as Roni Hirschenson, who have used their pain to drive them toward the suffering of their enemies. I have accounts of the tortures and brutalities committed by Israeli soldiers, as well as testimonies from Israelis who cannot stand what has become of their country. I have descriptions of the terrible damage done by suicide bombers, accounts of their hate-filled words, and biographies of some of their victims. But there is no point in listing more horrors. If the first Intifada brutalized both sides, the second left both sides traumatized, so much so that 10 percent of Israelis needed treatment for the same kind of shock that soldiers experienced in Vietnam and Iraq. Nothing good came of the uprising, so I have nothing more to add.

While the second Intifada only worsened the lives of Palestinians, the growth and expansion of the Jewish settlements in the West

Bank continues to poison Israeli society. The most aggressive settlers are not content with the land they have already grabbed, and they try to intimidate nearby Palestinians into moving away. For example, the settlers use rocks and even guns to drive Palestinians away from their own fields, so that they cannot harvest their olives. Some, like Dr. Shulman of Hebrew University, believe that they must push back against the settlers and stand up for the rights of Palestinians. They see this as their most basic obligation as Jews, as moral individuals: "Let no one say he did not know; let no one talk of vast historical forces, of wrongs piled on wrongs, of generalities and abstractions; let no one speak philosophy. What is real is this overriding anguish. It is in their faces; it is in my body; it is in these rocks and trees." While Israeli police and army troops too often either side with the settlers, or avoid clashing with them, Israeli judges have been more fair-minded, and have often upheld Palestinian rights. The fragile bond among activists such as Dr. Shulman, Palestinian farmers, and Israeli judges is the one sign of healing in the deep wound of occupation.

Although the Israeli–Palestinian conflict is always in the headlines, I actually do not think it is the central issue for Israel's future. That is because it is, as it always has been, an international problem. America, the United Nations, England, France, Russia, as well as predominantly Muslim nations such as Egypt, Saudi Arabia, and even Iran and Syria, have all contributed to the crisis and have been deeply involved in the negotiations. Surely whatever solution finally comes will be decided as much by all of these outside parties as by the Israelis and the Palestinians themselves.

If we leave the issues of occupation and peace treaties to international diplomacy and to the good will of individual Jews and Palestinians, what of Israel itself? How do the questions that came up earlier in Israel's history—about what it means to be a Jewish democratic state, about how American and Israeli Jews relate, about the rights of Arab citizens of Israel—look today?

WHICH ISRAEL?

I was in Jerusalem recently, speaking with teenagers at the high school that is connected to Hebrew University. This is one of the best schools in Israel, and I am certain some of the teenagers I met will become national leaders. These were brainy, articulate seniors, some within a month of starting their service in the army. I asked them what they would do if an officer ordered them to use force to evict Jews from the city of Hebron.

Hebron is the site of the cave in which Abraham is said to be buried. In that sense, the town is the very touchstone of Judaism in Israel. Yet Hebron is an Arab city in the land won by the Jews in 1967. And in Hebron a Jewish extremist named Baruch Goldstein, inspired by Kahane and his violent words, massacred twenty-nine Muslims in 1994. Jews are only able to live there today because they are constantly guarded by the Israeli army. Protecting the few hundred extremely religious Jews who insist on staying in Hebron both infuriates the Arabs and consumes the resources of Israel's army. In any final peace agreement between Israel and the Palestinians, the soldiers will surely leave, taking the devout Jews with them.

"I'd do it gladly," a tall, well-spoken boy said. "That is a battle I'd love to fight," added another, a solid, muscular kid who hopes to join the tank corps. But then a shorter boy with a tousled crop of dirty blond hair spoke up. "I live in Hebron," he said in a low, intense voice. "You'll never get us to leave."

This clash over Hebron is part of a larger conflict over what Israel is today. The kibbutzim are quaint and interesting to visit, and even inspiring in a way. But no one sees them as a model for the country. Today Dov and Hannah's kibbutz no longer harvests and sells fruit. Instead, money comes from the McDonald's franchise the kibbutz owns on a nearby highway. What, then, is the path for Israel? That choice became clearest to me at two places: the Wailing Wall in Jerusalem, and on the buzzing streets of Tel Aviv.

AT THE WALL

During our family trip to Jerusalem, Marina, my half-Indian wife, our two sons, and I went to see the Wailing Wall. Five-year-old Sasha kept asking to go right up to the wall because he had heard that you roll up prayers and stick them in the cracks between the stones. He had a message he wanted to send to God. But I kept feeling that I did not belong, that I was in someone else's territory.

The plaza in front of the wall is patrolled by women, such as the one who rushed up to my wife to scold her for not covering her arms. Was she more on edge because Marina has brown skin? Maybe, but Marina actually resembles many Mizrahi women, and the angry woman reminded me of similar guardians I've seen in Italian churches, in mosques, or, for that matter, the Alamo. Her job is to judge, to make sure every visitor obeys the rules. Sasha and I had to put on little paper skull caps, but that was not enough. A man called out to me, to offer me a prayer shawl and other religious items to wear. Huge signs face down above the plaza, advertising religious schools and teachers. Bearded men in black robes, rocking back and forth as they said their

A Jew praying at the Wailing (or Western) Wall in Jerusalem.

prayers, clustered along the base of the wall. A barrier clearly marked off the men's section of the wall from the women's.

The stern woman, the men lost in their intense devotions—the signs all said that this place belonged to the religious, the ultrareligious. The very air felt thick, choked with so many prayers, rules, and judgments that it was not meant for others to breathe. The wall was not for Jews in general, people in general, but for the devout. You should not be here, they were all saying, unless you are one of us. Sari Nusseibeh points out that the plaza itself was carved out by demolishing the Moroccan section of the city—one history swept aside to make space for another.

It was not always that way, even at the Wailing Wall, as the story of the early Zionists and their picnic here on Yom Kippur makes clear. Their Zionism had nothing to do with religious ritual. Today, ritual has taken over. "Why not?" one cousin asks. "The wall is their place, let them have it." But the possessiveness of the ultra-Orthodox bothers me. I feel that they don't just want the wall, but that they want to dictate how all Jews should live.

TEL AVIV

After a few days in Jerusalem, our family packed up a rented car and made the short drive down to Tel Aviv. Sometimes it feels like the greatest relief to be in Tel Aviv. You are in the twenty-first century, free to be yourself, an individual. You know that the people passing you by, speaking into their cell phones, are as up-to-the-second on trends in music, fashion, MySpace, Facebook, and YouTube as any teenager in America.

On a street in Tel Aviv, you see tattoos, even though they are forbidden under Jewish law, and were once particularly looked down upon because the Nazis tattooed numbers on prisoners in the camps. But you see them in Tel Aviv, along with whatever is the very latest men's, women's, straight, or gay fashion in Paris, Milan, Amsterdam, London, New York, L.A. Indeed, the lampposts sport posters for Gay and Lesbian Pride Week. Skyscrapers hem you in; cars whiz by; people look young and single; families with strollers huddle in parks, leaving the streets to the unattached. Tel Aviv is a beach city, and you feel that buzz of being young and alive all the more near the water. For all of the bikinis, monokinis, sunglasses there are in Tel Aviv, this could just as well be South Beach in Miami.

Tel Aviv is a relief because the rest of Israel is so laden with history and tradition. In Jerusalem, the Orthodox patrol the Wailing Wall. In Hebron the devout prepare for their battle against the Israeli army. In Tel Aviv the streets are filled with young people until sunrise. Trusted by their parents to be smart and self-reliant, teenagers, or small groups of them, are out on their own, enjoying the city. Is the future of Israel Jerusalem or Tel Aviv? This question reverberates through all of Israeli society, for it touches on the matter that you might assume would be central for a Jewish state: Who is a Jew?

THE QUESTIONS FOR A JEWISH STATE

Israel extends the right of return to anyone with one Jewish grandparent. But that only begs the question: What makes a grandparent Jewish? Worshippers at a synagogue in South India saw themselves as Jewish. A large group of dark-skinned Ethiopians thought of themselves as Jewish. After the end of the Soviet Union, some one million people who had never had the chance to practice any form of religion declared that they were Jewish, or married to Jews, or had Jewish ancestors. Eventually, and with some hesitation, Israel's rabbis agreed that all these peoples—the Indians, the Ethiopians, the Russians, and others—were Jewish, but those problems were easier to solve than the one posed by the moderate Judaism practiced by most Jews in Israel and America.

In 1950, the Orthodox rabbis argued that a Jew was only a Jew if born to a Jewish mother, or converted by an Orthodox rabbi. In America most Jews are Reform or Conservative, not Orthodox, and marriages to non-Jews are common. The Orthodox rabbis of Israel were telling Americans that their conversions or mixed marriages meant nothing. By 1960, Israel's political leadership agreed with the rabbis, because they needed their votes. But that did not settle the issue.

All Israelis carry identity cards, which at one time listed your religion. But what if you are a child of a mixed marriage, with a non-Jewish mother, or a mother converted by a Reform Rabbi? In 2002 the Israeli Supreme Court ruled that they should be listed as Jews. This so disturbed the government minister, who would have had to make the change, that the line for religion is now filled in with asterisks. In Israel, the Jewish state, the state itself is so unsettled about defining who is a Jew that it won't say anything at all.

And that leads to a major question about Israel: Does being a Jewish state strengthen or warp the country?

America is based on the idea of separating church and state. When Thomas Jefferson died, he left word that his tomb should honor his work for religious freedom as highly as the Declaration of

Independence. Today, if a town in the United States sets up a nativity display, soon enough there will be a court case, and either it will come down, or displays for one or several other faiths will go up near it. We may have a debate over evolution in one school or about reciting the words "under God" in another. But those debates are within a basic system of law that we all know: your religion (or your atheism) is your business. The nation, the state, is not there either to favor one faith or judge another. Government is one thing, religion is another.

Israel is based on the idea that one religion is essential to the state. That is part of why Israel feels so alien to me. Some people feel more at home, more planted where they belong, when they are among Jews all the time—from the ultra-Orthodox to the antireligious. That atmosphere of Judaism feels reassuring, nourishing. The presence of the group makes them feel more secure and more comfortable as individuals. I feel that too, every so often. But mainly I feel at home in a world of mixture, of interesting differences.

There is a bigger issue related to those emotions: Can a state be fully democratic and at the same time be linked to any one religion? Israeli law does not discriminate against non-Jews. Christians, Muslims, pagans, atheists do not have to pay a special tax; they can vote, run for office, plead a case in court. In fact, in some ways, non-Jews are less restricted in Israel than non-Christians are here. For example, while Jews are not allowed to buy pork in Israel, no one enforces the law, and non-Jews are exempt. In America, states that ban sales of alcohol on Sunday—church day—shut down all liquor stores. Still, my impulse is to say that a state tied to a religion cannot be fully democratic. After all, what happens if most people in the country change their minds and decide to demand strict religious practices, or if they choose to favor another religion or none at all?

For Israelis this is not an abstract question. Take the matter of the Israeli army.

Ben-Gurion saw the army as the key to the new nation of Israel. For that very reason it is, today, the most visible sign of the strains within Israeli society. Some extremely religious men—they can broadly be called religious Zionists—make it a point to serve in the army. But as of 2007, forty thousand draft-age religious men used the exemption originally granted by Ben-Gurion (which was revised and expanded in the 1980s to include many more religious students) to continue their studies and avoid service in the army. Forty thousand young men, in the prime of their lives, are exempted from being part of the "cement" that holds Israel together. In a small country that is a serious problem.

Dov's daughter Deborah served proudly in the Israeli army, as have her grown children. When I last saw her, one son was sitting in a tank on the border of Lebanon. Deborah was bitter about those religious students whose exemptions keep her son and sons like him in that tank. And not only are the religious protected from the risks she and her family have taken; her taxes pay for their huge families. The Israeli government gives families child support, and since the religious tend to have very large families, they get a disproportionate amount of government funding. With the ferocity of a mother whose son is in danger, Deborah demanded that the laws be changed, a sentiment that is heard over and over again from secular Israelis.

There is one other group that is exempted from the army: Arab citizens of Israel. The Israeli army admits some Arabs, Bedouins, and the Druze. But the majority of Israeli Arabs are not required to serve. Most do not want to, and they are not wanted. Would an Israeli Arab fire on his Palestinian cousin? Jews ask. Strangely enough, that means Israeli Arabs are in a similar situation to the forty thousand ultra-Orthodox who choose to study rather than be trained as soldiers.

Israel is in danger of pulling toward its extremes. That is a problem Israelis worry about, since the fastest-growing segments of the Israeli population are precisely those exempted from the army: the ultra-Orthodox, who want Israel to have much more restrictive religious laws, and the Arab citizens of Israel, who are not Jewish at all. When I met with high school students in Israel, they understood this demographic issue very clearly. One well-informed senior thought the government could manage the problem by finding private agencies to give support payments to Jewish mothers, who would then be paid twice: once by the government, once from a private fund. That way the government would be neutral, but the Jewish population would be nudged upward. Another senior was a typically pragmatic Israeli, who said, "When the problem comes, we'll deal with it." But other students were more puzzled and disturbed, unsure of how Israel could remain both Jewish and democratic.

Many Israeli teenagers, though, had a completely different reaction, which again might surprise American readers. They told me this whole question of Judaism and democracy was a false issue. They insisted that they identified themselves as Israeli, and being Jewish was a kind of flavor within that identity. "No matter where I am in the world," one told me, "I immediately know who is an Israeli. Even if we disagree on everything, we talk the same, we think the same."

Much of Israel shuts down on Saturdays, the Jewish Sabbath. But that does not mean most Israeli Jews are in synagogues praying. Instead, young people, like the ones I met, who feel more Israeli than Jewish, tend to use the day to visit with their families. The cousins from Jerusalem drive down to meet the cousins from Tel Aviv, and the cousins who live in Galilee, and the cousins down in the Negev. If Israel is Jewish, for many Israelis that means they are very close to their families, not that they pay any attention to Jewish laws. The shadow of the Holocaust and of Israel's wars is there even in those large families: Israeli Jews need life, new babies, the stories of elders, the buzzing, intrusive clan with its many feuds and personalities, to replace the memory of threat and death. Americans are much more spread out. We may chat online or gather together at major holidays, but cousins from California do not go to New York on weekends. We need our space (until we get lonely and look for a community to join); Israelis need their families (until they get claustrophobic and visit the rest of the world to be by themselves).

Israel cannot quite define what it is to be Jewish, and it will only resolve its borders with the help of other nations. So to bring together all of the questions that Israel raises for me, I turn back to the issue I began with, to those teenagers in Galilee and their swimming pool.

THE QUESTION ON WHICH ALL OTHERS REST

After our family trip to Tel Aviv, we returned to Jerusalem, then piled in the car again and set off to visit Tami, a cousin who lives in a hill-top settlement in a more northern part of Israel. The fastest way to get there is to take the number six, the superhighway that will one day run from one end of the country to another. As we sped along we started to notice a barrier running alongside, just outside our window. Sometimes it was far off, other times we drove quite close to it. For miles, the barrier was a fence topped by coils of barbed wire,

Sections of the wall erected to protect Israelis from Palestinian suicide bombers. As a security measure, the wall has been a success, but it also suggests a kind of walling off; the way an animal might grow a protective shell. Israel faces the challenges of protecting itself from determined, ruthless enemies while preserving its human face.

then a solid concrete wall. Every so often a watchtower jutted up from the horizontal span. Beyond we could just make out the rounded tops of Arab homes and mosques. We soon realized that we were driving right beside the wall the Israelis had built to keep out Palestinian suicide bombers. As a security device, the barrier has worked, although the Israeli Supreme Court ruled that parts of it must be moved as they are infringing on Arab access to their own lands.

Finally we arrived in Galilee. Tami's settlement is within the 1967 borders of Israel, but the houses were built by General Sharon as part of a plan to make that region of Israel less Arab and more Jewish. The settlements are very "liberal" in that they are open to many lifestyles. Single parents priced out of Tel Aviv can find nice homes there; nearby there is even one of the very few "integrated" schools in Israel, where Arab and Jewish children share classrooms and learn together.

At the bottom of the hills are Arab villages; the people who live there are Arab citizens of Israel. These are the families, and children of the families, who did not leave when Israel was born. They are called the "'48 Arabs," since they have been in Israel since 1948. In October 2000, in one of these villages, for the first and only time in Israel's history, Israel's Arabs erupted into riot and violence.

In fact, the real violence came from the Jewish side. The protests took place during the second Intifada, and were aimed against Israeli actions in the West Bank. Israeli police snipers shot and killed twelve demonstrators who were Arab citizens of Israel and one Arab who was not Israeli. In no other demonstration in Israel's history, no matter how violent, had the police shot people this way. The protest had been loud and angry before the police arrived, and one Israeli Jew was killed, when a demonstrator threw a rock from a bridge that hit a car passing on the highway. But this was not a riot. Still, the fury of the demonstrations terrified Jews. Here were a million people living within Israel, many of whom had close relatives among the Palestinians, and now they were angry, they were violent. Was this a new front for terror?

The official government commission that investigated the events of October came to the very opposite conclusion. The Israeli Arabs are Israeli. A retired Israeli military officer whose career was devoted to finding out the secrets of Israel's enemies, said, "I believe the situation between Israeli Arabs and Jews is one of this country's biggest success stories." The Arabs do not want to leave and join the Palestinians. They do not want to destroy Israel. They were driven to fury by the discrimination that they experience every day in employment, in housing, and in obtaining government support. There are too many Israeli Jews who will hire a fellow Jew and not even consider an Israeli Arab, even if he was more qualified for the job. Similarly, in 1968, a panel in America looked into the causes of the race riots in America's cities. The Kerner Commission warned that America was splitting into two societies, one black and the other white.

As an American, I believe that it is wrong to live in a segregated, divided society—here or in Israel. The Israeli government commission came to essentially the same conclusion. My cousin Tami's friend Itzi agrees. He is part of an organization named Sikkuy, which argues that Israel can only be Israel if its Arabs not only have legal rights (which they do), but are treated as full citizens (which they are not). Sikkuy was founded by another sabra, Shuli Dichter, who grew up on the same kibbutz as Willie Groag.

The Israeli flag is a Jewish star. "Hatikvah," the Israeli national anthem I quoted on page 21, is about the homeland for Jews. At soccer games, Israeli Arab teams cannot salute the flag of their own nation.

While these Israeli Arab boys jumping on a mattress near the Crusader fort at Acre (called "Acco" in Israel) look happy, they are poor, and making do with what they have. As I walked along the walls of the fort, I saw kids diving into the sea, and one was seriously hurt. Studies by the Israeli human rights group Sikkuy show that Israeli Arabs are, on average, one-third less well off than Israeli Jews.

Use the word "Israeli" in conversation and you surely mean "Jewish." These are some of the reasons why the Arabs prefer not to be called "Israeli," although, for some, it is also because they identify with other Arabs, not with Israeli Jews. But Itzi's point is larger: Israel needs to develop a broader idea of citizenship, of individual rights, and of what it means to be an Israeli in order to move forward in the twenty-first century.

In 2007, Sikkuy began publishing an annual survey, using official government statistics to compare how Israel's Jewish and Arab citizens fared in categories such as health, job opportunities, and education. They found that even though they are legally equal, a Jew is about one-third better off—similar to the advantage whites have over blacks in America.

The real challenge for Israel—the nation designed to be a homeland for the Jewish people, the land in which Jewish individuals feel strengthened by being part of a larger Jewish group—is how to make space for this growing group of non-Jewish Israeli citizens. This problem brings together all of the issues I have mentioned in this book. It is very much like the challenge America faced in the 1960s, during the civil rights movement.

Indeed, Shuli Itzi and his fellow activists remind me of civil rights workers in America. Here, Jewish rights are protected because all minority rights are protected. That is one reason Jews were so drawn to the civil rights movement: If discrimination against blacks was accepted, Jews might be next. If blacks were given greater opportunity, Jewish lives would be more secure. Sikkuy argues that the same principle applies in Israel. Only a society that fully and firmly protects its minorities can offer true safety to Jews. Then it would not matter if eventually 51 percent of the population were non-Jewish;

Jews would enjoy the same protections they had once extended to Arabs. Security comes from law and principle, not from numbers.

To be fair about this, Arab citizens of Israel are treated far, far better than a Jew would be if he or she lived in the lands of one of Israel's enemies. There is no Arab country in which Jewish rights would be protected by the courts, the way Palestinians have been in Israel. Still, Israel today is similar to America in Dr. King's time, a place where segregation is accepted as a way of life.

Itzi drove us from Tami's, down to a nearby Arab village so my older son could get a haircut and my wife and I could get some good coffee.

The streets of the Arab village Itzi took us to were narrow and cramped with cars. A lively crowd of high school girls swept by, all wearing light-blue shirts, dark blue skirts, and blazers, the kind of modest yet comfortable uniform you might see in an American Catholic school. Marina noticed that some of the girls ignored the dress code entirely and wore clothes that would have fit right in on the stylish streets of Tel Aviv. This was not the world of covered Muslim women you so often read about. Instead, I felt as though I were on Atlantic Avenue in Brooklyn, where for a few blocks the faces are Middle Eastern, some of the shop signs are in Arabic, but just past that is a Hispanic neighborhood, and then a gentrifying yuppie section. Walking through the village reminded me of how odd it is to be in Israel where Jews and Israeli Arabs are neighbors living in completely different worlds.

We wanted good coffee, which quickly became another symbol of the divisions between Jewish and Arab Israelis. In America, coffee is everywhere, and in whatever flavors or combinations you desire. In the Jewish part of Israel, we kept getting bad versions of Italian espresso or cappuccino. In the Arab village, there is no such thing as a coffee shop. Instead, we were told to go into a pastry store. Then, because the owner knew Itzi and liked him, he sent a boy to get coffee from his personal pot. To the Israeli Jews, coffee is a way to show they are part of Europe. To the Israeli Arabs, it is an expression of respect and honor; one serves it only when there is a personal connection. In Israel, even a cup of coffee is a marker of difference.

After we had our coffee and pastries, we went to the barbershop. As we waited for Sasha to get his haircut, we were having a lively conversation with Itzi, asking him about his work. A thin young Arab with black hair that hardly seemed to need a trim was seated next to us, wearing a leather jacket. We didn't assume he'd understand our English, but he did, and soon spoke up. He told us he lives in the village, and is studying in Haifa at the Technion, a kind of Israeli MIT that also has a medical faculty. He explained that the quaint old Arab homes in the village were wired and that the families are on the Internet all the time. And their children, like him, look forward to going to college. Indeed, in one branch of the Technion, 40 percent of the students are Israeli Arabs. But he also said they all want to return back to their villages after college, and live near their families. "We know we have to get an education," he said. "We don't know if there will be any jobs for us."

The conversation with the young man felt so familiar, we could have been speaking to a similar person anywhere in America. Marina kept remarking that you meet young people like him in immigrant communities all over America: close to their families, attached to their traditions, yet eager to go out into the modern world to be trained to get a better job. That blend of past and present felt so much more normal and familiar to me than the choice between ultrareligious

Jerusalem and ultramodern Tel Aviv. In that brief conversation, I felt I was back home.

Later, we drove the short distance back up the hill to the Jewish settlement. There I heard the story about the Arab Israeli who had to go to court to be allowed into the local swimming pool. When I met with that class, I was looking out at faces I might have seen at many American high schools. The teenagers had just about any style of hair or dress that would be worn in a typical suburb here. In the hallways they were on their cell phones or listening to their iPods. One girl, tired of the stereotypes she had heard when she visited America, urged me to tell American teenagers that Israelis don't have camels and are not always dodging bombs. In that lively modern classroom, those American images of Israelis sounded particularly ridiculous. The teenagers were so familiar. Yet they were also different. Take the matter of dating.

I asked what they felt about dating the Arabs who live just down the road. Not one was willing to consider it. But then I asked about dating a dark-skinned Jew from Ethiopia. They were all perfectly open to the idea. The borderline of black and white, which is still so strong in America, was invisible to the Jewish teenagers. One way to see the role religion plays in Israel is to think of what race means here. You could say that the whole arc of American history since the civil rights movement of the 1960s has been the final acceptance that being "white" does not make you any more "American." And that is the step I believe Israelis—Jews and Arabs—need to take: realizing that being Jewish does not make you more Israeli (or being Arab, any less).

The teenagers spoke of the Arabs as alien people with whom they had nothing in common. I saw the wall go up: the hardening that has come from real Arab threats, and the intense Zionist drive to build a

Jewish state. As a practical fact, the wall we had driven by is a necessity. But walls have also become part of the Israeli state of mind, and they seal in as much as they seal out.

In Jerusalem I heard a very cultured Israeli man say, "Arabs are a different race from us," which, in terms of science, is almost funny. Israelis, especially those in the West Bank settlements, openly speak of Arabs in the most derogatory ways, saying, for example, "Arabs are worms." Or "It is well-known that Arabs have been slaughtering and murdering Jews for more than a generation. I think it is in their blood. It is something genetic." Right next to those settlements, Palestinians are watching TV shows, listening to radio broadcasts, reading newspaper articles that are equally, if not more, false and vicious in describing Israeli Jews. The language of hate is spoken on both sides.

This is the kind of talk that makes Israel feel alien to me. No matter how comfortable I feel with Israelis in one moment, the next I hear attitudes that, like the order Jeffrey Goldberg was given in Ketziot, remind me that I am American. We are just as prejudiced as they are, and they may well be more honest. But all too often they simply accept their rigidity, their walls, as facts. They have grown comfortable with separation, not mixture.

When Israelis speak of Arabs—or Muslims, in general—as fundamentally different, they sometimes point to recent tensions around Muslim communities in France, Holland, or England. Not one of them ever brings up the obvious counterexample: Muslims have lived in North and South America ever since the days of Columbus. They have raised families, earned their livings, joined in the political processes of their nations. Nothing about their religion or culture has marked them as fundamentally "different" from any other citizens. After the terrorist attacks on September 11, 2001, Muslims in

America came under intense scrutiny. To my knowledge, not one has been shown to be disloyal. No Israeli Jew even tries to explain how that history fits with their description of Muslims as so different they must be excluded or kept apart.

The will, the absolute determination that built Israel, has meant that Israeli Jews see others only out of the corners of their eyes. There they always loom as threatening, completely alien, so totally different that the only sensible thing to do is to remain entirely separate. In America, for all of our prejudices and problems, we have gotten used to the exceptions. We are quick to put people into racial boxes, but we all also know about the black chess club, the Asian NFL player, the white rapper, and the Jewish author who is conflicted about Israel. We are used to getting a taste of one another's worlds. That fluidity is what is missing in Israel.

The Jews are blunt and direct, so their positions are clear, and for all I know, when they speak in private, the Arab citizens of Israel have similarly harsh judgments of their Jewish neighbors. At times Itzi spoke of the Israeli Arabs the way Americans sometimes do about American Indians, as if they were a pure, traditional people who should be left to their ancient ways. That sounded odd to me, especially for a wired village whose children are rushing off to college. Perhaps it was his way of hinting that as much as the Arabs demand to be treated as equal citizens, they prefer to stay separated from the Jews. The wall serves both sides.

Indeed, on December 31, 2006, the leaders of the Arab communities in Israel issued a "Vision Statement" about how they saw the future. They wanted Israel to change fundamentally, to be a state of two distinct peoples, not a Jewish state. They wanted the flag and the anthem to change, and even the schools. Many Israeli Jews were offended, alarmed. To them this seemed like proof: The Arabs are Arabs, they will never accept being part of Israel. Yet other Israelis have pointed out that in an official statement, political leaders often take strong positions, while in polls the majority of Arabs in Israel want to get along, with less discrimination and more opportunity.

This desire pits the Arabs against Israel's largest wave of recent immigrants, the Russians.

THE RUSSIAN ISRAELIS

When my grandfather moved to Tel Aviv, three of his children remained in Russia. Because of the tension between the Soviet Union and the United States, we received almost no information about them and their families. But in 1964, the American government sent my father back to Russia as a visiting artist. When he arrived in the Soviet Union, he was desperate to see his sisters. Everyone told him that was a bad idea. Too many Russian Aronsons had been executed or sent to Siberia by the Communists, so an American showing up would only put the family in more danger.

But my father could not be stopped. He went to the apartment house where one sister lived and ran up four flights of stairs to see her. Whether it was because he was sixty-six, or because of her insistence on keeping the door sealed shut, he suffered a heart attack and needed to be rushed out of the country.

Many years later, I finally met the children of my Russian relatives at Dov and Hannah's kibbutz. After the end of Communism, they made it out, along with some one million other Russian Jews and their families. Those Russian Jews are cultured; many are accomplished musicians and scientists (we have some in the family)—warm and bright people. When they reached Israel in the 1990s, they rushed into the army, often taking on the most dangerous assignments.

The Russian Jews cannot stand the Arabs, whether they are Arab Israeli or Palestinian. Some experts think this reflects a strong anti-Muslim streak in Russia, which battled against the Mongols centuries ago; others point to intense discrimination Jews suffered in Russia, which fills them with a fire to strike back at anyone who looms as a threat to Jews. Because the Russians are newcomers, they have no experience living near Arabs, so they have no friendships with Arabs to moderate their biases. Whatever the deep causes, the Russian Jews are completely intolerant of Muslims. Sitting at dinner with my wonderful relatives—who suffered so much under Communism, who have so much to give the world—you would think you were in the American South in the 1940s. Arabs, they say, are dangerous, should not be allowed into Israeli society, and should be cleared out of Israel.

Because they served in the army, these most recent immigrants, many of whom are not even Jewish, have become fully Israeli. Yet the Arabs they detest, who have lived in Israel since it was born (and in their villages long before that), are somehow marginal to Israel. I am sure there is some rough parallel to recent Hispanic immigrants in America, who volunteer for military service because it is their best option for getting schooling and a good job, yet who face discrimination. But the prejudice you hear against Arab citizens of Israel, especially from the Russians, is much more extreme than anything directed toward Hispanics—at least in public in the last fifty years.

I spoke about all of this one day with a Hispanic police officer here in New Jersey. She sympathized with the Israeli Jews' desire to seal off from all threats. "Look," she said, "I've been on patrol in very tough cities at the time of year when the Bloods and Crips are initiating new members into their gangs. We know that one way to qualify for joining a gang is by killing a police officer. When I'm walking those streets, I am as tense, as on guard, as those Israelis."

HOW CAN AMERICANS HELP ISRAEL?

When Israel was fighting wars and coping with uprisings, we in America had it easier. Although our soldiers have been in harm's way, and we went through one terrible day of terrorism, we have not faced the dangers the Israelis experience all the time. Only a few of us, like that police officer, spend each day knowing they are the targets of armed men.

Our safety gave us an opportunity. We have had the chance to go through the civil rights movement, to face our prejudices and to accept that we live in a shared nation. We have had the luxury of letting down our guards a bit, and to become more comfortable with difference. I want to say to those Jewish high school students and those Arab Israelis: You can make your Israel, your nation, greater. The more each of you can see that Israel is both of you—Jew and Arab—the stronger Israel will become.

The point is not just about Arab citizens of Israel. Rather, what I heard in those young people is how Israelis build their walls higher. They keep turning back to what they know—how to be strong, smart, determined, and focused. As an outsider I want to say, make some space for those outside the walls. Begin to see those others not just as aliens or enemies but as part of your own landscape. I don't know how the Israelis can do that, nor is it my place to tell them how. But I can see the price they pay for being enclosed. That is the benefit I have of looking at them from my place of safety.

You can see that need to open up in Israelis just after they get out of the army. Those self-reliant young people scatter to every continent. So many of them go to India that Gidi's daughter and her husband (who married in Las Vegas because they are so nonreligious), own a restaurant in the foothills of the Himalayas that sells Israeli home cooking to the waves of backpackers coming through. Every year, Kathmandu, the capital city of Nepal, fills up with Jews at Passover, who gather there for a massive meal hosted by an Orthodox group.

Young Israelis need to get away from their tiny, claustrophobic country and touch every inch of the planet. In that way, they are much more open to the world and more curious than the many Americans who never go overseas. Americans have the good fortune of being able to explore the world by visiting the homes of their classmates, or wandering through the ethnic neighborhoods in any city. Israelis live in a Jewish state and need to rush out to visit everywhere— anywhere—else.

Many organizations, such as Birthright, bring American teenagers to Israel to see the country, to visit historic sites, and to meet Israelis. Writing this book for American teenagers made me realize that those same teenagers also have a vision to bring to Israel.

American teenagers have grown up with Black History month, with the "I Have a Dream" speech. They have grown up in an America that is increasingly Hispanic and Asian. I believe Americans have something to tell the Israeli young people they meet: It is possible to have a different form of nationalism, patriotism, Judaism. Israelis like to quote American rabbis who fear that because of intermarriage,

Judaism will disappear in America. Indeed, in a recent survey of young Jewish Americans, the majority said that for them, "Judaism is more of a cultural issue" than a matter of specific religious practices. But that is very similar to the Israeli teenagers I interviewed, who identify more with being Israeli than being Jewish. In fact, Judaism is in no greater danger of dissolving in one nation or the other. So the openness of American Jews to other Americans is something Israelis need to learn about, just as they need to hear how Americans react to their walls and prejudices.

Ever since the first aliyah, Jews have had to choose: America or Israel. The Israelis built a beautiful Jewish homeland. Americans found a way to live among strangers and to feel at home. Today, home and homeland are deeply linked. Maybe that is the model we Jews can offer the world: not nationalism behind walls, not an internationalism in which you lose yourself, but an ebb and flow between the two that allows for both. If we merely "stand with" Israel, we are like a guilty parent who pays off a neglected child with gifts, and so prevents him or her from maturing. We deny Israel our insights and our understanding of how it can grow and change. That is not support. If we treat Israel as a Jewish theme park and not as a real nation shared by people of different faiths and backgrounds, we are using the country for our purposes and not helping it to face its own challenges.

Three weeks after we left Israel in the summer of 2006, the Middle East erupted into war. Hamas and Hezbollah were each deliberately provocative, launching rockets and kidnapping Israeli soldiers. Israel responded with a massive air attack on Lebanon, and an invasion with ground forces. The Israelis relied on their greatest strength, the air force, which has been their ace since 1967. But this time it did not work. After the conflict, Hezbollah was, if anything, stronger than before. And throughout Israel there was great distress, both because war aims had not been achieved and because Israel was creating so much death and destruction for so little gain.

Hamas and Hezbollah are real threats to Israel. Deborah's son in the tank at the Lebanon border, as well as two of Shlomo the landscape architect's sons, saw action in the fighting. A few bombs landed near Dov's kibbutz; Tami and her kids, as well as many other relatives I haven't mentioned by name, had to move to safety as rockets struck near their homes. We discovered later that all were fine. David Grossman is one of the best-known authors in Israel, and he was not as fortunate. His son Uri served in the Israeli army, and was killed on the last day of the fighting in Lebanon. When he was finally ready to face the public, Mr. Grossman urged Israelis to put away their blinders. "Just once," he insisted, "look at them [the Palestinians] not through the sights of a gun, and not behind a closed roadblock. You will see there a people that is tortured no less than us." Maybe, just maybe, in small ways, we visiting Americans can use our experiences in battling our prejudices to help that happen.

Israel has done the impossible in building a beautiful land. Assuming that Iran's nuclear program is brought under control, it will continue to exist for as long as anyone can see ahead. But the idea of Israel was never simply to have land with borders and an army. It was not to be an island fortress. Israel was meant to offer hope—to Jews, and, really, to all human beings. It was meant to be a place where people could live better lives. For the Israel of hope to exist, Israeli Jews face a different challenge. The Jews need to learn how to live with fellow citizens who do not share their religion, do not share their history, and do not share their culture. The test of the Israel of hope is to keep its human face when dealing with its Arab citizens, while being strong in facing Arab threats; to make space for ultra-Orthodox beliefs, while insisting that Orthodox men serve the country that sponsors and protects them; to end the occupation, with safe borders.

Israel's existence is a political fact. But what it means to be Israeli is debated on every street corner and Israeli website. That is good. It is healthy. Those who insist that to question Israel is to be disloyal, anti-Semitic, self-hating are wrong. Israel is a changing home in a changing world, which means that Israel is real: not a dream, not a gift of God, not a perfect place. It is a beautiful, unsettling land. Questioning—even arguing with God—is what makes Israel live.

THE PICTURE QUESTION

When I first thought of creating this book, I wanted it to be full of pictures. I wanted to share the Israel I have seen—in person and in history books—with you. I asked my cousin Ari Aronson, an experienced photo researcher and photographer, to help me. But even as Ari hunted down aerial shots of Tel Aviv and historic images of battles and such, I began to change my mind. These photos seemed to clash with, to chop up, a text that read more smoothly without them. So we stripped down the list to just a few iconic beats in the story. Maybe someday I'll do a photo essay on Israel with Ari, but that is another book.

PHOTO CREDITS

A NOTE ON SOURCES

I have known about Israel all of my life, and have been involved with it through family, visits, or reading as far back as I can remember. So you could say that I researched much of this book before I knew I would write it. The stages of my reading about Israel probably match those of many engaged, liberal American Jews.

When I was growing up, the one book on Israel you were sure to find in every Jewish home from its publication in 1958 and on was Leon Uris's novel *Exodus*. This is a heroic story based on a real incident in which you are meant to root for the Jews. Today the style and ideas in the book are strikingly dated. But if you speak to any adult who has not kept up with scholarship on Israel, their view of the events of Israeli independence may well still be grounded in this novel. My own first semifictional exposure to Israel came through James Michener's *The Source,* which I truly loved for combining archaeology, history, and the land of Israel. I went to Israel not long after having read it, and seeing *tels*—mounds containing ancient shards—much like the one he wrote about, was a real thrill. I knew about Israel in pictures as much as in text. Teddy Kolleck was a popular mayor of Jerusalem, and his book *Jerusalem: Sacred City of Mankind* was the kind of gorgeous photo essay you would also see in Jewish homes. Photo-filled books showing the archaeology of Israel by authors such as Yigael Yadin were also commonplace, as were Robert Capa's marvelous photos of the '48 war and the founding of Israel. Abba Eban's *My Country: The Story of Modern Israel* would likely sit beside these coffee-table books.

All of these books were written entirely from a Jewish-Israeli point of view. They were moving, even inspiring, and heroic. But they were incomplete. One way to think of this phase of writing about Israel is to think of books and movies about the American West. In the '50s and '60s, TV shows, films, even textbooks and biographies, were excited about the way west—the spirit of freedom, independence, and democracy was expressed through the stories of white men and their families. Blacks were invisible, Indians were savage or doomed, "half-breeds" were sinister, Mexicans were lazy and/or cruel, and Chinese were exotic extras. Only after the civil rights revolution of the later 1960s did the story change. On the one hand, the white pioneers were shown to have less than admirable and democratic attitudes; on the other, we began to include African American soldiers and sodbusters, American Indian heroes, Mexican vaqueros, and Chinese railroad workers in the pageant of the West. The same shift came a decade or so later in writing about Israel. Howard M. Sachar's *A History of Israel*, which first came out in 1976 and is now in its third edition, was critical of the rise of the ultrareligious Jews. In the 1980s and '90s, Israeli historians, such as Benny Morris and Tom Segev, begin to question and undermine the entire thrust of the old histories of Israel. This led to furious conflicts among Israeli historians, much like the arguments among Americans over how to tell our history.

The problem is that while, in Israel, that old heroic story was being chipped away, for many Americans it was still unchallenged. In fact, as advocates for Israel and the Palestinians appeared on TV, each told half the story so that instead of Americans learning about how Israeli Jews themselves were reexamining their past, we were asked to choose: sabras as either heroes or villains. In a sense, my goal in this book is to share with Americans the debates about Israel's past, present, and future that take place within Israel itself. For many American adults, Thomas Friedman's highly readable *From Beirut to Jerusalem* allowed them to begin questioning the occupation.

When I came to write this book, I decided that I could skip the first two phases of writing about Israel: the heroic books, and then the doubters. I could still remember the books I grew up reading, and I knew the arguments raised by later critics. So I decided to pick up with the debate as it is today.

I went to a few bookstores and cleaned out their shelves of books on the Israel–Palestine issue. Many of those offered useful summaries of the history leading up to the present. The titles of the books show both their similar focus and a hint of their differing perspectives. The books I used most frequently included James L. Gelvin, *The Israel–Palestine Conflict* (hereafter IPCG); Gregory Harms, *The Palestine Israel Conflict* (hereafter PICH); Dan Cohn-Sherbok and Dawoud El-Alami, *The Palestine–Israeli Conflict* (hereafter PICCE); and Alan Dowty, *Israel/Palestine* (hereafter IPD).

All of these books were written as college-level surveys. They lay out the issues and, either by having advocates from each side (as in PICCE) or by summarizing similar views found elsewhere (as in the rest), attempt to be as evenhanded as possible. I found Gelvin and Dowty to be the most useful; Professor Gelvin was helpful in an exchange of e-mails, as was Dr. Dowty, who generously read this entire book. When the books conflicted, or I was not satisfied with their conclusions, I did further research, often by looking for more specialized articles on the Internet. I suggest a similar strategy to my readers: If you want to know more than I tell you, check out books like these. Beyond them, you can use online search engines, because you will have a good background for evaluating the often bitterly opposed sites they yield.

Baruch Kimmerling, who passed away while I was writing this book, was an Israeli scholar who had been called a post-Zionist. He was fully Israeli, but did not agree with his country's brand of nationalism. I found his *The Invention and Decline of Israeliness* both provocative and engaging, although my cousin Shlomo the historian emphatically disagreed. Two books fashioned around interviews with modern Israelis were exceptionally helpful to me. I strongly recommend both of them to any interested reader: Donna Rosenthal, *The Israelis* (hereafter IR); and Arthur Neslen, *Occupied Minds* (hereafter OM). Two books by American Jews, whose years of experience in Israel left them with many questions and criticisms, helped sharpen my sense of being an engaged outsider/insider: Richard Ben Cramer, *How Israel Lost* (hereafter HIL); and Jeffrey Goldberg, *Prisoners* (hereafter P). Sari Nusseibeh's memoir *Once Upon a Country* (hereafter OUC) gave me access to the insights and observations of an exceptionally thoughtful and informed Palestinian; my editor, Ginee Seo, alerted me to David Shulman, *Dark Hope* (hereafter DH), a moving account of the struggle people of conscience face in opposing the bullying and prejudice of settlers in the occupied territories. For general background information, I used Paul Johnson, *A History of the Jews* (hereafter HJ). Although aimed at adult readers, Gershom Gorenberg's *The Accidental Empire: Israel and the Birth of the Settlements, 1967–1977* is a readable guide to the tangled history of the settlements that a motivated teacher could use with high school students.

If you go the English-language website of the Israeli newspaper *Haaretz*, www.haaretz.com, you can keep up with all current issues in Israel. *Haaretz* is distinctly more "liberal" and "secular" than it is nationalistic or religious. But the paper eagerly solicits e-mail "talkback" to its columns—those reader comments bring in a wide spectrum of Israeli views, and are easy to find on the site. To learn more about Sikkuy, or to get updates on its efforts to track the comparative status of Jewish and Arab citizens of Israel, go to www.sikkuy.org.il.

I am intensely aware of what I did not read: the shelves full of studies of Israel and of Palestine, the books arguing forcefully for or against either side, any books at all in Hebrew or Arabic. I urge any motivated reader who thinks he or she can punch holes in my arguments by doing that extra level of research to do exactly that.

NOTES

Sources listed in the bibliography below are referenced in short form (by the author's last name and key words from the title). Frequently cited sources are referred to by abbreviations of their titles, as explained in "A Note on Sources," on page 166.

FOREWORD

p. 5 For the statistics on land ownership, see Bernard Avishai's *The Hebrew Republic*, pages 25–26.

p. 7 For "violence of heart and mind," see DH, page 10.

p. 9 For one chilling example of a French comedian whose comedy is based on raving anti-Semitism, see Tom Reiss, "Laugh Riots," *The New Yorker*, November 19, 2007. The article is available online at http://www.newyorker.com/reporting/2007/11/19/071119fa_fact_reiss.

INTRODUCTION

pp. 11, 13 See http://www.imemc.org/news_articles/palestinianattacks.

I. HOW DID ISRAEL COME TO BE?

p. 16 Mark Twain, *Innocents Abroad*, chapter 56.

p. 19 For the national anthem of Saudi Arabia, http://david.national-anthems. net/sa'.htm; for Poland and Denmark, among others, go to http://www. lyricsondemand.com to search through the many national anthem lyrics this site makes available.

p. 19 For Abraham, see Genesis 12 (King James Version).

p. 20 For the DNA tests, see "Jews and Arabs Are 'Genetic Brothers,'" BBC News, May 10, 2000, http://news.bbc.co.uk/2/hi/science/nature/742430.stm.

p. 21 This translation of "Hatikvah" can be found in OUC, page 31.

pp. 21–23 For Herzl, see HJ, page 396.

p. 27 For Wilson and the self-determination of peoples, see IPCG, pages 85–87.

p. 28 For "the world . . . safe for democracy," see Link's *Woodrow Wilson and the Progressive Era, 1910–1917*, page 281.

p. 28 For Balfour, see IPCG, page 81.

p. 29 The Ottoman plan is described in Johnson, *The Birth of the Modern*, page 690.

p. 29 For "sacred trust," see IPCG, page 86.

pp. 30, 32 For this paragraph on oil, see Yergin, *The Prize*, an award-winning history of oil. The book is long but filled with profiles of fascinating characters, and any motivated high school student can easily read it. (Also see Curzon, page 183; Balfour, page 189). For a quick Internet introduction to the history of oil, see "Extreme Oil: The Evolution of a Valuable Resource," Thirteen/WNET New York, http://www.pbs.org/ wnet/extremeoil/history/index.html.

p. 38 See HIL, page 146, in which Cramer is quoting from a book by a prominent Israeli author.

p. 42 For the quotation from the Reform Jewish school text, see P, page 53.

p. 42 "Boycott" and "sell" can be found in IPCG, page 99.

p. 43 Readers who want to know more about Neolin, Pontiac, and the

Proclamation Line can read my *Real Revolution: The Global Story of American Independence* (New York: Clarion Books, 2005).

p. 47 I found these details about Ford in the author's note to Philip Roth, *The Plot Against America* (New York: Hougthon-Mifflin, 2004). The book is fiction, but the note spells out the actual events behind the alternative history Roth invents. For "leaky boats," look up that phrase along with "Charles Coughlin" in any search engine: one site I found was the Holocaust Chronicle's "1938: The End of Illusions," http://www.holocaustchronicle.org/StaticPages/147.html.

p. 49 I am grateful to Russell Shaw, middle school director of the Abington Friends School, for this insight on how the debate over Israel is essentially one over the Holocaust.

p. 52 I learned of Marie Groag's experience in the kibbutz from her daughter, Eve.

p. 53 Information on Hannah Senesh, including the translation of her poem can be found at http://www.hannahsenesh.org.

p. 56 For the extract from Anwar Nusseibeh's diary, see OUC, page 48.

p. 62 Any reader interested in history—and interested in Israel—should read up on Deir Yassin. It is a great example of how stories change, and are used by different sides, and take on lives of their own. I found the article "Deir Yassin: The Conflict as Mass Psychosis," archived at http://www.mideastweb.org, to be helpful, and the e-mail storm it generated was fascinating. Readers might want to start with HJ, IPCG, or IPD to get oriented, then venture out on the Web to see the spins different groups put on the events. To get the story of the Palestinian refugees as Israelis used to tell it before Benny Morris, see Leon Uris's novel *Exodus* (New York: Bantam, 1983). Morris himself is doubly controversial. On the one hand, some Israeli Jews take strong issue with his relentless digging to expose the crimes their soldiers committed against Arabs in 1948. On the other hand, more recently, his views have changed. While not denying any of his scholarship, he now feels that, as a pragmatic fact, it would have been better if all of the Arabs had left Israel, or had been forced out. That position infuriates "liberal" Israeli Jews, as well as almost all Israeli Arabs. But no matter the storms that swirl around Dr. Morris, he has led the way in bringing forth new evidence about the events of 1948.

pp. 64–65 For Anwar Nusseibeh on his mistakes, see OUC, page 57.

p. 66 For Dina Peleg, see OM, page 181.

p. 68 For Jefferson's letter in which he makes the famous "wolf by the ear" statement, see Digital History, http://www.digitalhistory.uh.edu/documents/documents_p2.cfm?doc=399. Teachers will also find the following page especially useful, including the last link on the page, which leads to the Digital History site with the Jefferson letter, http://www.pbs.org/wnet/slavery/teachers/lesson2.html. For the Duke Ellington quote, see Alex Ross's *The Rest Is Noise*, page 154.

p. 72 For more on this poll, see IPD, page 197.

p. 73 For Abu Ramsi, see HIL, page 102. For Sari Nusseibeh's speech in Israel, see OUC, page 167.

II. ISRAEL IS BORN—WHAT IS ISRAEL?

p. 81 For Ben-Gurion on the army, see Hazony, *Jewish State*, page 274.

I found this to be a useful, informative, college-level background book.

pp. 84–85 For Ben-Gurion on bringing American Jews to Israel, and the response from the American Jewish Committee, see Wheatcroft, *The Controversy Over Zion*, page 250. This academic text will be of most interest to teachers, but it contains interesting quotations like these, which you don't find in more general histories.

III. DID WINNING THE 1967 WAR RUIN ISRAEL?

p. 93 For *The Voice of the Arabs* radio program, see OUC, page 87.

p. 95 I learned a great deal about the Six Day War in Oren's *Six Days of War*. This is a wonderfully well-researched and well-written book that makes gripping reading for anyone from a high-school age and up who is interested in these events. For the president of Iraq, see *Six Days of War*, page 164; for the head of the PLO, see *Six Days of War*, page 132; for the loudspeakers, see *Six Days of War*, page 189; for the lieutenant, page 97; and for Israel's prime minister, see *Six Days of War*, page 169.

p. 101 For General Mitza, see OM, pages 218–19.

p. 102 For Sari's view of the Old City in 1968, see OUC, page 109.

p. 103 The "three no's" are mentioned in any book on this period; see, for example, IPD, page 117.

p. 107 For Golda Meir on the nonexistence of the Palestinians as a people, see OUC, page 172.

p. 109 For Ben-Gurion on Mizrahi Jews, see OM, page 4.

p. 110 From Gorenberg, *Accidental Empire*, pages 358–64.

p. 114 Abba Eban's comment can easily be found by using any search engine; one webpage I found was Buzzle.com's "Abba Eban," http://www.buzzle.com/editorials/11-17-2002-30508.asp.

p. 117 For the saddened Israeli commenting on the shift to "taking care of number one," see OM, page 56.

IV. CAN ISRAEL OCCUPY CONQUERED LANDS AND BE TRUE TO ITS IDEALS?

p. 121 For "amputees of the soul," see OM, page 169.

p. 125 For Goldberg's experience at Ketziot, see P, pages 116–17.

p. 127 For Dov Yirma, see OM, page 49.

p. 127 For Roni Hirschenson, see OM, page 194.

p. 128 For "misjudgment of reality," see P, page 254.

p. 129 For the assassin's reasons, see IPCG, page 237.

p. 133 For more on the al-Aqsa Martyrs Brigade, see "Profile: Al-Aqsa Martyrs' Brigades," BBC News, July 1, 2003, http://news.bbc.co.uk/2/hi/middle_east/1760492.stm.

V. HOW CAN ISRAEL BE A STRONG STATE, A JEWISH HOMELAND, AND TRULY DEMOCRATIC?

p. 136 For Dr. Shulman's plea for seeing the suffering of Palestinians, see DH, page 112.

p. 149 For the retired intelligence officer's optimism, see OM, 262.

p. 151 For the report on Jews and Arabs in Israel, see *The Sikkuy Report: The Equality Index of Jewish and Arab Citizens in Israel*, 2006 edition. This can be downloaded online at http://www.sikkuy.org.il/english/en2006/Table_of_Contents.pdf.

p. 154 For more on the history of race in America, see my book *Race: A History Beyond Black and White* (New York: Simon & Schuster, 2007).

p. 155 For slurs on Arabs from settlers, see OM, page 241.

p. 161 The survey is quoted in Shmuel Rosner, "In U.S., Some Write Their Own Mezuza Prayer, Others Turn to Torah-Yoga," Haaretz, January 18, 2008, http://www.haaretz.com/hasen/spages/946063.html.

p. 162 I first heard about David Grossman's speech from Naomi Shihab Nye, who mentioned it in her talk at the 2006 ALAN breakfast. I am grateful to her for the reference. I found the full text on the Haaretz site, http://www.haaretz.com/hasen/spages/784034.html.

BIBLIOGRAPHY

This is a listing of books, many of them quite recent, that I found helpful in writing *Unsettled*.

Avishai, Bernard. *The Hebrew Republic: How Secular Democracy and Global Enterprise Will Bring Israel Peace at Last.* Orlando, FL: Harcourt Brace, 2008.

Ben Cramer, Richard. *How Israel Lost: The Four Questions.* New York: Simon & Schuster, 2004.

Cohn-Sherbok, Dan, and Dawoud El-Alami. *The Palestine–Israeli Conflict: A Beginner's Guide.* Oxford, U.K.: Oneworld Publications, 2003.

Dowty, Alan. *Israel/Palestine.* Malden, Mass.: Polity Press, 2005.

Gelvin, James L. *The Israel–Palestine Conflict: One Hundred Years of War.* Cambridge, U.K.: Cambridge University Press, 2005.

Goldberg, Jeffrey. *Prisoners: A Muslim and a Jew Across the Middle East Divide.* New York: Knopf, 2006.

Gorenberg, Gershom. *The Accidental Empire: Israel and the Birth of the Settlements, 1967–1977.* New York: Times Books, 2006.

Harms, Gregory. *The Palestine Israel Conflict: A Basic Introduction.* London: Pluto Press, 2005.

Hazony, Yoram. *The Jewish State: The Struggle for Israel's Soul*. New York: Basic Books, 2000.

Johnson, Paul M. *The Birth of the Modern: World Society 1815–1830*. New York: HarperCollins, 1992.

———. *A History of the Jews*. New York: HarperCollins, 1988.

Kimmerling, Baruch. *The Invention and Decline of Israeliness: State, Society, and the Military*. Berkeley, Calf.: University of California Press, 2001.

Link, Arthur S. *Woodrow Wilson and the Progressive Era, 1910–1917*. New York: Harper & Row, 1954.

Neslen, Arthur. *Occupied Minds: A Journey Through the Israeli Psyche*. London: Pluto Press, 2006.

Nusseibeh, Sari. *Once Upon a Country: A Palestinian Life*. New York: Farrar, Straus & Giroux, 2007.

Oren, Michael B. *Six Days of War: June 1967 and the Making of the Modern Middle East*. Oxford: Oxford University Press, 2002.

Rosenthal, Donna. *The Israelis: Ordinary People in an Extraordinary Land*. New York: Simon & Schuster, 2003.

Ross, Alex. *The Rest Is Noise: Listening to the Twentieth Century*. New York: Farrar, Straus and Giroux, 2007.

Shulman, David D. *Dark Hope: Working for Peace in Israel and Palestine*. Chicago: University of Chicago Press, 2007.

Wheatcroft, Geoffrey. *The Controversy Over Zion: Jewish Nationalism, the Jewish State, and the Unresolved Jewish Dilemma*. Reading, M.A.: Addison-Wesley Publishing, 1996.

Yergin, Daniel. *The Prize: The Epic Quest for Oil, Money & Power*. New York: Simon & Schuster, 1993.

ACKNOWLEDGMENTS

I knew that in writing about Israel I ran two big risks: I could get some fact or interpretation wrong; and even if I made no mistakes, I might infuriate people whose life depends on telling their own version of this story. Indeed, for many issues about Israel there is no clear and commonly agreed upon right and wrong. That is why I am exceptionally grateful to the expert readers who read all or part of the manuscript, and helped guide me in my work. Thank you to Dr. Dowty, whose thoughtful review of a draft manuscript saved me from several errors; to Dr. Ronald W. Zweig, Henry and Marilyn Taub Professor of Israel Studies in the Skirball Department of Hebrew and Judaic Studies at NYU, for your comments and corrections; to Dr. David Commins, for his thoughtful review of the book from the point of view of an expert on the Arab and Muslim Middle East; to Carl Perkal and Ali Haider—both are officers of Sikkuy, but their points of view are quite different; Dr. Saul Fisher, Ari Aronson (if you ask an Israeli to find photos, he will also tell you what he thinks of your book), and Rita Auerbach also all gave me very helpful criticisms and comments. Bruce Feiler, a friend of a friend, was generous in responding to questions on Hebron. Although I found the views of all these commentators helpful, I alone am responsible for the ideas, facts, and conclusions in this book. No reviewer had a veto on what I would say, so no reader should infer that what I say here reflects the views of any of the people I have named.

Thanks to the many Israeli teenagers who spoke with me, and to all of the Aronsons and Groags who hosted us in Israel. I have not listed the interviewees by name, date, or place, but all of the discussions took place in June 2006. Thank you to Emily LaVerriere, for reading this book in manuscript stage and giving me the insights of one particularly bright (non-Jewish) American teenager. Amy Berkower and Ken Wright at Writers House have helped, in ways small and large, to make this book possible. I am so glad they keep reading, talking, and thinking about how to make my books better.

Thanks to Jeannie Ng, for being meticulous and painstaking in ways that make the book a much cleaner read, and to Michael McCartney, whose smart design has made the book a pleasure for me to look at every time I pick it up.

As ever, my wife Marina was a great editor, helping me through endless drafts. This was the first young adult book of mine that my son Sasha was able to read, and it was thrilling to get his questions and comments on the pages he read. This book is dedicated to Ginee Seo, who had the vision, guts, and brains to make it happen.

INDEX